COMPUTATIONAL THINKING FOR PRESCHOOLERS

Nurturing Creative Thinkers & Problem Solvers

Joohi Lee

National Association for the Education of Young Children
Washington, DC

National Association for the Education of Young Children

1401 H Street NW, Suite 600
Washington, DC 20005
202-232-8777 • 800-424-2460
NAEYC.org

NAEYC Books

Senior Director, Publishing & Content Development
Susan Friedman

Director, Books
Dana Battaglia

Senior Editor
Holly Bohart

Editor II
Rossella Procopio

Senior Creative Design Manager
Charity Coleman

Senior Creative Design Specialist
Gillian Frank

Creative Design Specialist
Ashley McGowan

Publishing Business Operations Manager
Francine Abdelmeguid

We would like to thank General Motors for their generous support toward the development of STEM-focused initiatives, including this book, *Computational Thinking for Preschoolers: Nurturing Creative Thinkers and Problem Solvers*.

Library of Congress Control Number: 2025934307

ISBN: 978-1-952331-03-9

Item: 1175

Contents

CHAPTER 5

About the Author

Joohi Lee, PhD, is professor of early childhood mathematics education in the Department of Teacher and Administrator Preparation at the University of Texas at Arlington (UTA). With nearly 20 years of dedicated service at UTA, Dr. Lee has been instrumental in preparing preservice and in-service teachers for excellence in early childhood education, especially in early childhood mathematics pedagogy courses. Before joining UTA, she worked as a classroom teacher and early mathematics consultant, experiences that continue to inform her teaching and research. Her primary research interests focus on early mathematics education, teacher education in early childhood, and children's computational thinking. Additionally, Dr. Lee explores innovative intersections of coding and robotics with children's logical-mathematical and computational thinking.

Dr. Lee actively supports her local community by conducting workshops for teachers of young children that focus on mathematical thinking, computational thinking, coding, and robotics, as well as by serving on the math committee for local schools. She has an impressive record of scholarly contributions, with over 50 refereed articles published in leading journals and numerous presentations given at local, national, and international conferences. Dr. Lee is also the author of *How to Teach Math to Children* (Cognella Academic Publishing, 2016), currently in its second edition, further establishing her as a thought leader in early childhood STEM education. Her work continues to influence researchers, educators, and young learners, advancing knowledge and practice in the field of early STEM education.

Acknowledgments

I would like to express my heartfelt gratitude to my mother, Eunboon Lee, whose unwavering belief in my ability to thrive as a scholar in early childhood education has been a constant source of inspiration. Her encouragement and faith in my journey have sustained me throughout this writing process. I am also deeply grateful to my sister, Dr. Joo Ok Lee, a fellow researcher and educator in early childhood education. Her simple yet powerful reassurance of "You can do it" has stayed with me in moments of doubt and determination alike. Sharing this field with her has deepened my appreciation of the significance of publishing with NAEYC and its impacts on our profession. Her quiet prayers and steadfast support have uplifted me more than words can express.

My brother-in-law, Dr. Moon Soo Kim, has offered invaluable prayers, encouraging me to remain diligent in my work. My nephews, Yechan and Yesung Kim, have been joyful and uplifting supporters, even in their twenties. I also honor the memory of my father, Reverend Soon Wong Lee, whose deep passion for early childhood education helped shape my path. Though he passed away 15 years ago, his legacy lives on in me and continues to inspire me every day.

I extend my sincere thanks to my editor, Rossella Procopio, whose encouragement, meticulous feedback, and thoughtful edits have been instrumental throughout this process. I am also grateful to Dana Battaglia, NAEYC's director of books, for believing in this project and supporting my vision from the very beginning.

This book would not have been possible without the spiritual, emotional, and practical support of my family and the guidance of these incredible individuals. I hold deep gratitude for each of them.

Introduction

As an educator and researcher, I have spent years exploring how to integrate computational thinking (CT) into early childhood education in ways that feel natural and meaningful to young children. One evening, I had a conversation with my neighbor—a computer scientist and father of two daughters, ages 4 and 5—about the idea of CT for preschoolers. His initial reaction was one of surprise, and he asked, "Really? Isn't that a bit early?" This simple question kicked off an engaging hour-long exchange of perspectives. We discussed what CT really means—things like breaking problems into steps, spotting patterns, and figuring out how to solve challenges. I described how young children learn these concepts through play, stories, and hands-on exploration, and he shared how those same ideas show up in computer science. The longer we talked, the more we realized we were speaking the same language. By the end of our conversation, my neighbor smiled and said, "You know, I never thought of it that way, but it makes perfect sense." That moment reminded me how universal CT skills really are—and how powerful it can be to start nurturing them in the preschool years.

When hearing the term *computational thinking*, many people immediately associate it with computing numbers, computer science, or programming.

Skepticism about CT in early childhood is not uncommon. When hearing the term *computational thinking*, many people immediately associate it with computing numbers, computer science, or programming. Critics often argue that CT is too advanced, abstract, or inappropriate for young learners. My neighbor voiced similar concerns, questioning how concepts from a technical domain could be meaningfully adapted for children ages 3 to 5. Some early childhood educators also share this viewpoint, perceiving CT as complex and disconnected from the developmental realities of young children. This initial hesitation is completely understandable and often stems from limited information about CT, as well as a lack of clear examples demonstrating its applicability in early learning settings (Lee, Joswick, & Pole 2023; Lee & Junoh 2019). On the other hand, some teachers are eager to integrate CT but feel somewhat intimidated by the term itself and the uncertainty about where to start or how to effectively incorporate it into their teaching (Lavigne, Orr, & Wolsky 2022).

When approaching CT for young children, the first step is to understand that, while closely interconnected, computational thinking is not the same or interchangeable with computing, computer science, or programming. CT is a cognitive framework for problem solving. It falls under the umbrella of computing and is integral to computer science and programming, which is a branch of computer science. Figure I.1 visually illustrates this relationship.

Figure I.1 The Relationship Among Computing, Computational Thinking, Computer Science, and Programming

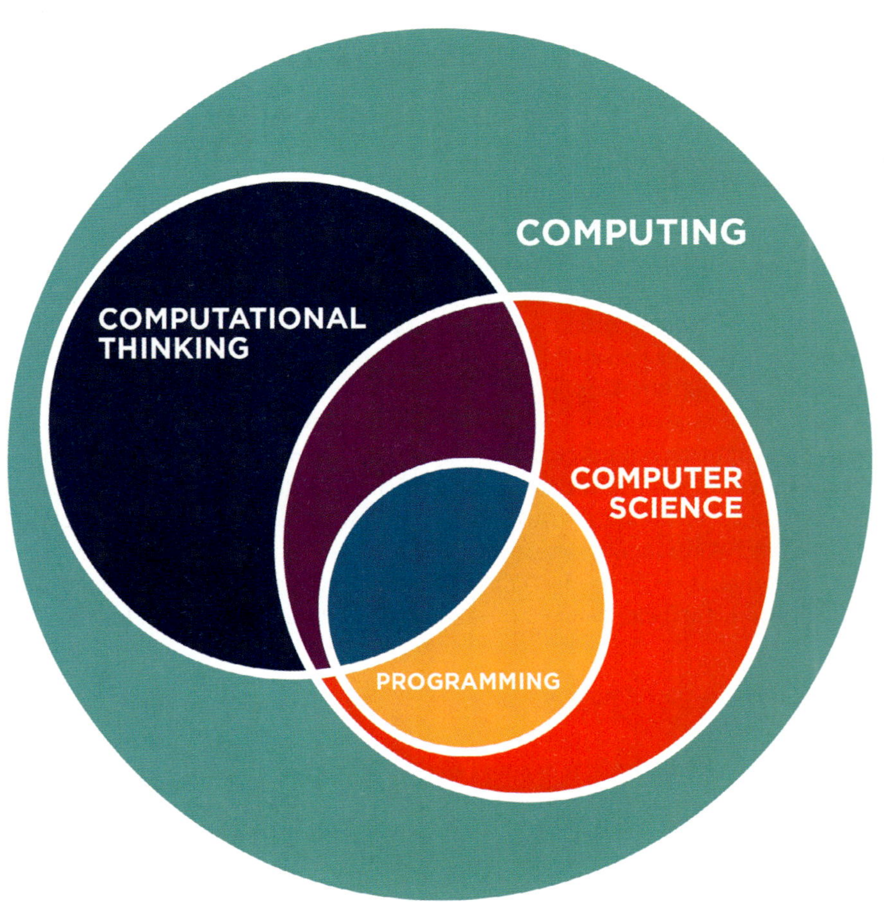

Adapted, by permission, from K. Mills et al., *Computational Thinking for an Inclusive World: A Resource for Educators to Learn and Lead* (Digital Promise, 2021), 9.

CT is also an independent skill set that leverages concepts that overlap with computer science and can be applied more broadly to problem solve in other contexts and academic disciplines. In other words. CT is not limited to any specific field or to individuals pursuing careers in computer science—it is a universal skill set for everyone. CT equips children with the ability to think logically, analyze problems, and develop solutions systematically, making it an essential competency for navigating the complexities of our increasingly digital society.

CT is not limited to any specific field or to individuals pursuing careers in computer science—it is a universal skill set for everyone.

Who Is This Book For?

This book discusses the importance and benefits of integrating computational thinking in young children's learning and provides core information and practical strategies to support teachers in this effort. It is designed specifically for teachers of children ages 3 to 5 who are not familiar with computational thinking or are unsure about how to begin integrating it into teaching and learning. This resource serves as both an introduction and a guide, offering educators foundational knowledge about CT concepts and skills while connecting them to existing practices.

My goal in writing this book is to make this topic accessible and practical. It demystifies CT by breaking down complex ideas into simple, actionable steps that teachers can immediately apply in their early learning settings. Whether you're a seasoned educator looking to expand your teaching strategies or a newcomer excited to explore innovative ideas, this book provides examples and approaches tailored to help young children think creatively and solve problems effectively. It empowers educators to foster children's CT in natural, everyday contexts and introduce targeted CT learning experiences to further support and deepen children's CT development.

Imagine a vibrant early learning setting buzzing with curiosity, where every question, every game, and every playful moment becomes a stepping stone toward building powerful CT skills. If this describes the kind of learning environment you would like to create for children, this book is for you.

About the Book

The contents of this book are organized into five chapters.

Chapter 1 sets the stage by defining what computational thinking is and outlining its origins. After tackling some common myths surrounding the concept of CT, it briefly overviews the four major CT skills—decomposition, pattern recognition, abstraction, and algorithmic thinking—and how they work in the problem-solving process. It also offers a glimpse into CT's application in early childhood education. This chapter serves as your gateway to a deeper conceptual understanding of CT.

You'll dive into the heart of CT with **Chapter 2.** Following a discussion about CT's connection to children's cognitive and social and emotional development, the four major CT skills are explored more closely. The underlying key concepts for each skill are brought to life with examples familiar to the early learning setting. Additionally, you'll gain a better understanding of how these skills overlap with one another. This chapter also offers practical pedagogical strategies, including guidance on the types of questions educators can use to ignite children's curiosity and deepen their understanding.

From morning circle time to building block structures to navigating obstacle courses, the routines and play-based learning experiences that young children engage in every day inherently incorporate computational thinking. **Chapter 3** explores how teachers can intentionally foster CT learning already happening in their setting with an emphasis on technology-free, or unplugged, learning experiences. It also highlights how to integrate learning experiences that directly target CT skills and concepts. Packed with hands-on activities and illustrative vignettes, this chapter helps teachers to weave CT seamlessly into their teaching and learning.

Coding is one of the most powerful methods to develop CT in children, and stories provide the perfect framework to make its concepts both meaningful and fun. **Chapter 4** takes you step-by-step through the process, from selecting stories to navigating coding grids. In addition, the chapter highlights key terminology to integrate into your interactions with children and ideas for extending this learning experience.

Finally, **Chapter 5** is your road map for continuing your journey as a teacher who recognizes the value of CT in the early learning setting and beyond. Structured around three calls to action, it offers educators approaches and strategies to keep learning, growing, teaching, and advocating.

With this book, step into the exciting world of CT in early childhood and discover how to nurture the next generation of creative thinkers and problem solvers!

CHAPTER 1

Computational Thinking in Early Childhood

Thought Questions

- What exactly does computational thinking entail in the context of early childhood education?
- Why is it important to incorporate computational thinking into early childhood learning?

Computational thinking (CT) has recently gained widespread popularity in the field of education, becoming essential for all students to thrive in today's digital society (ISTE 2019). This skill set has also captured the attention of early childhood educators and researchers, who recognize the importance of providing children with opportunities to practice CT from an early age (Bers et al. 2014; Joswick et al. 2023; Lee 2020; Papadakis, Kalogiannakis, & Zaranis 2016). Because of its potential to significantly enhance children's problem-solving abilities and educational journeys, CT is increasingly being embedded across various curricula (ISTE 2019).

CT represents a mindset that extends beyond computer science, coding, programming, or simply interacting with technology. It embodies skills that play a critical role in shaping how children think, plan, and problem solve (Papert 1996). Moreover, CT has been shown to positively influence children's attitudes toward learning and to support development in other domains besides the cognitive (Relkin, de Ruiter, & Bers 2021; Pila et al. 2019). For instance, it improves hand–eye coordination through engagement with manipulative objects and enhances executive function and learning behaviors like self-regulation (Bers et al. 2014; Yang, Luo, & Su 2022; Yang, Ng, & Gao 2022).

As interest in CT grows, many early childhood educators question what exactly CT is, what it involves, its necessity in early childhood, and how to effectively integrate it into early learning practices. This chapter presents a foundational understanding of CT, including its definitions and origins; addresses common misconceptions about CT; briefly reviews major CT skills; and illustrates its potential application in the preschool setting.

What Computational Thinking Is and Its Origins

There are many definitions of computational thinking provided by researchers and educators alike, but none is currently universally adopted. That said, there are similarities across the various definitions that can be drawn on to create a shared understanding.

A commonly accepted definition of CT in the field of education is a thinking process that involves problem solving. It is characterized by analytical strategies that often apply computer science principles and techniques, including but not limited to decomposition, pattern recognition, abstraction, and algorithmic thinking (Barr & Stephenson 2011; Grover & Pea 2013; Wing 2006). Simply put, CT is not about thinking in the same way a computer does; rather, it's about leveraging computational methods and approaches in the human problem-solving process.

CT is not about thinking in the same way a computer does; rather, it's about leveraging computational methods and approaches in the human problem-solving process.

Tracing the origins of CT reveals that its roots extend back to at least the 1950s, though many of its foundational ideas are much older. CT encompasses numerous principles (e.g., abstraction, data representation, the logical organization of data) that are also integral to other forms of thinking, including scientific, engineering, systems design, and model based. Early computing pioneers like Alan Perlis and Charles Thornton (1960), as well as Donald Knuth (1972), introduced and promoted terms like *algorithmizing, procedural thinking, algorithmic thinking,* and *computational literacy* to help distinguish and conceptualize CT, explain its core ideas, and highlight its importance as a problem-solving approach that is applicable across disciplines. However, the term *computational thinking* was first introduced by Seymour Papert in 1980 and reiterated in 1996. During this time, CT was interpreted as a tool to algorithmically address complex problems and was often used to achieve goals and make significant improvements in efficiency (Papert 1980, 1996).

The phrase *computational thinking* gained broader recognition within the computer science education community in 2006 when Jeannette Wing published her influential essay framing CT as the essence of problem-solving capabilities. Wing (2006) defined CT as a set of analytic skills involving problem-solving processes that enable individuals to navigate complex challenges, both in academic contexts and daily life. She argued that CT is a fundamental skill for everyone, not just computer scientists, and emphasized the importance of integrating CT into various school subjects for all students. Wing also suggested that CT could improve children's ability to perform everyday tasks requiring systematic thinking and the execution of logical steps. This perspective has been embraced in education, significantly influencing instructional practices and promoting the integration of CT into a wide range of content and learning environments.

Today's perspective of CT aligns closely with the one put forward by Wing. It is recognized as a comprehensive problem-solving framework that does not belong to a specific academic field. Instead,

CT serves as a versatile cognitive tool for addressing challenges, fostering innovation, and enhancing problem-solving abilities across disciplines and professional contexts (ISTE & CSTA 2011; Wing 2008). As a result, CT has gained significant visibility and is now identified as an imperative skill for the twenty-first century (ISTE 2019). Furthermore, it is well agreed upon that all children should acquire and practice CT skills, just as they learn reading, writing, and math (ISTE 2019; Wing 2006).

Debunking Myths About Computational Thinking

There are many myths about CT, which can hinder its effective integration into learning environments, especially in early childhood education. Understanding and debunking these myths is crucial for educators to appreciate the value and applicability of computational thinking in their teaching practices. What follows are some widely perceived misconceptions and counterarguments to each.

Myth: Computational thinking is only relevant for computer science.

Reality: CT extends far beyond the boundaries of computer science, or "the study of computers and algorithm processes, including their principles, their hardware and software designs, their applications, and their impact on society" (Tucker 2003, 6). It encompasses the whole problem-solving process and thinking skills that are fundamental to various forms of learning and everyday life. For young children, this means developing the ability to think logically, recognize patterns, and approach and solve problems in a structured and creative way. These theoretical skills are invaluable to children's daily experiences and across all areas where problems occur, not just in computer science.

Myth: Computational thinking is just for programmers.

Reality: A programmer's main work is to create and develop functional computer programs to perform specific tasks, or programming (Dale & Lewis 2019). However, CT involves more than programming; it develops critical thinking and creativity, which are valuable for young learners. Introducing basic, developmentally appropriate CT concepts in early childhood education—like creating simple step-by-step instructions (algorithms) for daily routines, tasks, or problems—lays a strong foundation for logical thinking and creative exploration (Lee et al. 2022). This approach helps children understand the world around them by applying their CT skills, not just in a programming context.

Myth: Computational thinking is too complex for young children.

Reality: Young children are naturally curious and are already engaging in basic forms of CT in their daily lives, especially when they experiment, explore patterns, and try to solve problems. Learning experiences like sorting objects, following directions, and engaging in simple games that involve sequences (e.g., Simon Says) are practical, age-appropriate ways to introduce computational thinking.

Myth: Computational thinking is just another subject to teach.

Reality: Rather than being an isolated subject, CT can be integrated into various aspects of the curriculum across grade levels (ISTE 2019; Wing 2006). It enhances existing subjects by providing a new perspective and approach to problem solving using CT-associated analytical skills. For example, in mathematics, computational thinking supports children in creating simple repeating patterns with blocks. In literacy, children can tap into these skills to break down stories into smaller parts by identifying major events.

Myth: Computational thinking requires advanced technology.

Reality: Many assume that computational thinking necessitates high-tech gadgets or software. This myth likely arises from the viewpoint that CT is only for computer science or programming (Wing 2006). However, at its core, CT is a mindset that can be cultivated without any technology. For instance, tech-free (or unplugged) learning experiences like sorting objects by shape or navigating an obstacle course can effectively foster CT in young children (Lee 2020).

At its core, CT is a mindset that can be cultivated without any technology.

The myths reviewed here and more like them often arise from misconceptions or a lack of understanding about CT's fundamentals. By debunking these myths, teachers of young children can focus on the core principles of CT and effectively integrate them into their practices.

Major Computational Thinking Skills and Their Use in Problem Solving

When considering computational thinking, the emphasis should be on the thinking process itself. This approach challenges educators to focus on helping children to be aware of and understand how they think and solve problems. By analyzing the components of CT, teachers can identify strategies to enhance children's CT skills. To provide some initial grounding, the major CT skills are briefly defined in this section. Chapter 2 provides more in-depth exploration and analysis of these four principal CT skills:

- **Decomposition** is the process of breaking down a big or complex problem into smaller, more manageable parts.
- **Pattern recognition** involves identifying similarities and recurring elements among data, problems, or scenarios.
- **Abstraction** is the ability to generalize from specific instances and focus solely on relevant information, ignoring unnecessary details.
- **Algorithmic thinking** involves creating step-by-step instructions or rules, also known as algorithms, to solve problems.

Figure 1.1 Example of the Computational Thinking Process to Solve a Problem

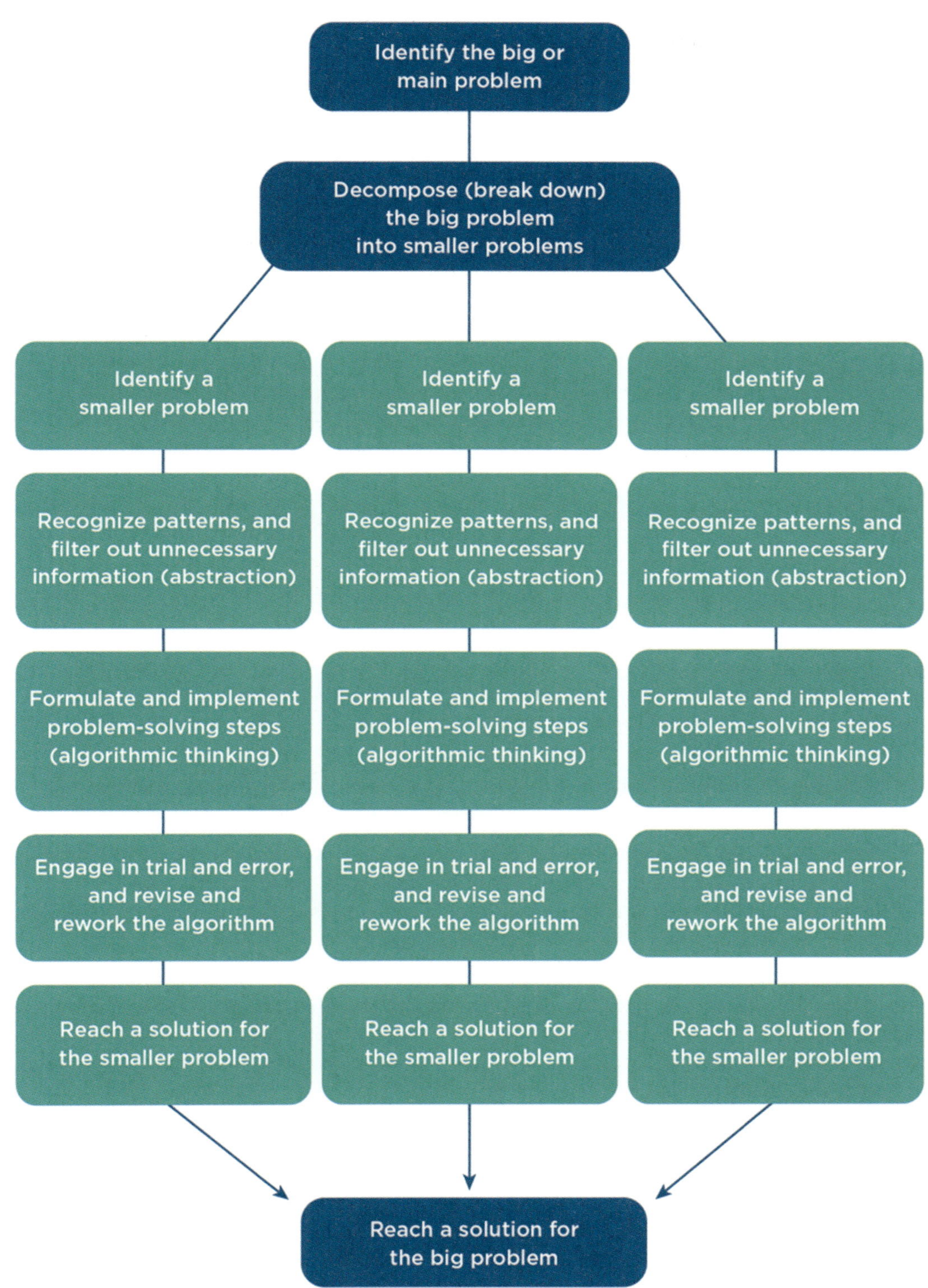

These skills are fundamental to children's computational thinking, providing them with the necessary tools to analyze and solve problems efficiently. By practicing these skills, children become more effective problem solvers that are capable of applying CT principles to a wide range of tasks and challenges. This, in turn, prepares them for navigating the challenges of our increasingly digital and information-driven world.

Figure 1.1 illustrates how these CT skills are involved in problem solving; specifically, it represents an example of the computational thinking process. While this example provides a basic framework for approaching and solving problems, it is important to note that the sequence of steps may vary. The CT process to problem solving can differ depending on a child's cognitive development, skills, and experiences; the complexity and context of the problem; and other factors.

The steps in this framework are explored further here:

- The very first and most important step in this process is to **identify the big or main problem** at hand. Crucially, this involves fully understanding what the problem is and what needs to be solved.
- Next, **the big problem is decomposed or broken down into smaller problems** to make it easier to solve (Relkin, de Ruiter, & Bers 2021). This step is implemented if the big problem is complex enough to require breaking it down into more manageable parts to resolve it. If necessary, children can further break down these smaller problems into even smaller parts for easier management. If the original problem is already simple and within children's capability to tackle directly, decomposition might be skipped. Decomposition is one of the four major CT skills.
- Once **the smaller problems are identified,** each is solved individually by employing the logical reasoning and analytical thinking skills overviewed in subsequent steps.
- As children begin the process of solving each smaller problem, they look for recognizable patterns. Additionally, this step requires abstraction to ensure that their attention is only directed toward the relevant aspects of the problem. Pattern recognition and abstraction are two of the four major CT skills.
- From here, children practice **algorithmic thinking,** which involves creating and carrying out step-by-step solutions, or an algorithm. Algorithmic thinking is one of the four major CT skills.
- Throughout the problem-solving process, children **engage in trial and error,** which entails experimenting with various strategies to determine those that lead to the most effective and efficient solution. Trial and error often involves debugging tasks, meaning oversights, mistakes, or other issues within a solution are identified and corrected.
- When a particular strategy does not produce the desired outcome, children **revise the algorithm,** exploring new paths toward a possible solution by exploring alternative methods or eliminating ineffective components. This iterative process not only helps in finding the solution but also enhances adaptability, as children learn to navigate challenges and adjust their strategies based on the outcomes they observe.
- Once the smaller problems are solved, children combine their solutions to address the big problem. This step means that children **synthesize the outcomes from each smaller problem to form a comprehensive solution to the big problem.**
- Finally, children **evaluate their solution to the big problem,** ensuring that it effectively resolves the issue and meets the intended goals. If necessary, they revisit earlier steps to refine their approach, demonstrating the iterative and flexible nature of the CT process.

The CT process offers a simple yet flexible way for preschoolers to approach problem solving. It helps young children think creatively and tackle challenges in ways that feel achievable and fun. By practicing these steps, they not only solve problems effectively but also build confidence and important thinking skills for the future.

Computational Thinking in Action in a Preschool Setting

Children engage in CT in their everyday classroom learning experiences and routines at various levels, even if it isn't explicitly acknowledged by their teacher. However, without intentional teacher scaffolding and guidance, these experiences may not fully support the development of children's CT skills. By observing and deconstructing children's play and learning experiences, teachers can identify and nurture these emerging abilities. The following scenario, based on an observational note from a learning setting for preschoolers, illustrates this point. Without a clear understanding of what CT looks like in an early childhood education setting, the following might be categorized merely as a science activity or an inquiry-based task. However, it closely aligns with the principles of CT and has the potential to enhance children's CT skills, depending on the teacher's perception and guidance. Examine the details to see if you can identify elements of CT.

Mr. Crowley's Class Digs for Earthworms

Mr. Crowley is observing the 3- and 4-year-olds he teaches while they play outdoors. He notices a small group of children deeply engrossed in digging through the playground soil with shovels. Curious, he heads over and asks what they are doing. The children enthusiastically fill in Mr. Crowley about their search for earthworms. The excitement reaches its peak when one of the children, Maggie, discovers an earthworm, shouting joyfully, "I found the earthworm, I found the earthworm, I found it!"

The other children gather around to see Maggie's find as she proudly shows the earthworm. Motivated by this discovery, another child, Ezra, declares, "I want to find one too." Grabbing a nearby shovel, he begins to dig in the sandy area beneath the monkey bars. Two more children, Mia and Nina, quickly join in digging through the sand. This soon sparks a wider interest among the children, with several others beginning to dig and explore different areas of the playground. It is not long before excited shouts fill the air as some children announce their success in finding more earthworms.

If the children's search for earthworms is considered a "problem" or challenge, it can be analyzed in the context of a problem-solving process. Some of the CT skills that can be observed in this scenario are identified here:

- **Decomposition.** The first stage of the process involves breaking down the overall challenge of finding earthworms into smaller, more manageable tasks. This might include identifying potential locations for earthworms, selecting appropriate tools for excavation, and the act of digging itself.
- **Algorithmic thinking.** After breaking down the task of finding earthworms into smaller components, the children use algorithmic thinking to create a plan that follows a logical sequence (Lee et al. 2022; Lee & Junho 2019). For example, children might start by scoping out likely earthworm habitats, then obtain a shovel, and finally dig at their selected site. While there is a general structure, some flexibility exists. Some children, for instance, might choose a trowel before pinpointing a specific spot to dig. Additionally, children might outline a specific procedure for each task. For instance, using algorithmic thinking to acquire a shovel could involve a series of steps: head to the storage area, select a suitable tool for digging, grab a shovel, and proceed to the intended digging location.
- **Pattern recognition.** Through observation of and interaction with their peers, children may begin to notice patterns related to earthworm behavior and habitat. They might, for instance, observe that earthworms are often found in moist, shaded areas of soil or learn through conversations that earthworms are more active during certain times, such as early morning or after rainfall. By recognizing these patterns, children can apply this knowledge strategically. For example, they might focus their search on areas of the playground that align with the earthworm's preferred environments, or they may time their search based on their understanding of when earthworms are most likely to be near the surface. This application of pattern recognition helps children approach the task of finding earthworms more efficiently.
- **Abstraction.** Instead of being distracted by the variety of plant life—a detail that, while interesting, does not directly impact the presence of earthworms—children learn to focus their attention on environmental factors that correspond to the presence of earthworms. These factors may include the moisture level of the soil, which earthworms prefer for the ease of movement and availability of food it provides, and the soil's depth, as earthworms are often found deeper in the soil where moisture is retained. By applying abstraction, children assess the environment based on these key criteria. For example, they might prioritize searching in shaded areas where the sun has not dried out the soil or choose to dig in areas where the soil appears loose, a condition that typically supports a healthy earthworm population. This focused approach not only increases their chances of finding earthworms but also teaches children an important problem-solving skill.

As you can see, daily learning experiences and routines in early childhood education naturally incorporate CT skills. This is particularly true of tasks that require step-by-step procedures, such as washing hands, tying shoelaces, and brushing teeth. As an educator, it is important to identify opportunities for CT within children's play and recognize how CT can be intentionally integrated into familiar learning experiences. These moments allow teachers to purposefully support children's CT development through practice. (For more examples of CT and its four major skills in action in a preschool learning environment, see Chapters 3 and 4.)

In taking on the role of a guide and facilitator in this earthworm-finding activity, you have the opportunity to help children cultivate and refine their CT skills. You empower them to become more adept problem solvers by thinking logically and systematically across a spectrum of contexts, ultimately fostering effective problem-solving abilities that are applicable in various facets of their lives.

The excitement of searching for earthworms provides a playful and meaningful opportunity for children to practice their CT skills while they remain engaged and enthusiastic. Although this learning experience doesn't involve technology, it gives children a real-world context to develop and use CT principles. This example reflects the natural ways in which children engage in problem solving as part of their everyday lives. As an observant educator, you can notice when children use CT and intervene to further develop these skills.

Creating Teachable Moments to Address Challenges

When children face challenges with problem solving, these can become teachable moments to actively engage children in using their computational thinking skills. These opportunities not only help children overcome the immediate difficulty, they also promote creative thinking and flexibility in addressing future challenges. Several strategies can support this process, each of which is explored here using the earthworm search as a specific example to illustrate their application:

- **Encourage trial and error.** For children who have not yet succeeded in finding earthworms, consider allowing them to continue their search independently or with a partner. This approach nurtures resilience, promotes exploratory learning, and emphasizes the importance of learning from mistakes—key elements in effective problem solving. Encouraging children to reflect on and understand why an attempt didn't work can help them gain insights into earthworm habitat preferences, such as their need for moisture and specific behavioral patterns. This reflection helps children refine their strategies.
- **Stimulate inquiry through discussion.** Engaging children with open-ended questions like "Where do you think earthworms might live?" can spark curiosity, promote hypothesis development, and encourage creative thinking. For example, Mia may suggest that earthworms live in sandy areas. When Ezra points out that he didn't find any earthworms in the sand, Maggie might add that she found an earthworm near a tree. These types of discussions promote inquiry-based thinking, allowing children to apply logical reasoning to their methods and refine their understanding collaboratively.
- **Promote peer collaboration.** Encouraging children to seek insights or assistance from peers who have already found earthworms can be highly effective. This approach fosters teamwork, enabling children to share strategies and experiences. As children learn from one another and build on their collective knowledge, they also develop their cognitive and social and emotional skills.

By fostering a learning environment where trial and error, inquiry, and collaboration are encouraged, educators can promote essential skills that extend beyond CT and problem solving. These strategies nurture an adaptable mindset, confidence, curiosity, and interpersonal skills, all of which are critical for children's long-term growth and success as well-rounded, competent learners (Relkin, de Ruiter, & Bers 2021).

> When children face challenges with problem solving, these can become teachable moments to actively engage children in using their computational thinking skills.

Enhancing Children's Success in Problem Solving

Once children successfully solve a problem, you can further enhance their CT skills. Here are a few approaches to consider, again illustrated with the scenario of finding earthworms:

- **Recognize success.** Positively acknowledging when a child finds an earthworm can boost their confidence and motivation. Celebrating small achievements helps children experience the joy of accomplishment and reinforces their continued curiosity and willingness to try new things.
- **Promote reflective inquiry.** Guide children to think critically about their decisions, actions, and outcomes. Through open-ended questions and comments, teachers can prompt children to articulate their strategies (e.g., "How did you decide where to dig for the earthworm?"), engage in self-assessment of their approaches (e.g., "What do you think worked well?," "What challenges did you face?"), and consider the outcomes of their actions (e.g., "I wonder why you didn't find an earthworm in the sandy area"). This strategy encourages children to more deeply analyze their problem-solving process and develop a better understanding of what they learn.
- **Facilitate sharing and collaborative learning.** Motivating children to share their methods for discovering earthworms with their peers can significantly enhance the learning experience for everyone. Sharing might involve discussions about specific tactics, such as targeting moist soil areas or adopting a strategy that worked for another peer. Such exchanges not only enrich the group's collective understanding of effective problem-solving strategies but also highlight the importance of diverse approaches. Additionally, peer-to-peer teaching fosters a sense of collaboration, allowing children to learn from one another in a supportive and interactive way.

By implementing these strategies, educators celebrate individual achievements and leverage these successes to foster a collaborative, reflective, and enriched learning environment. This reinforces the computational thinking skills of individual children while extending these benefits to the entire group, promoting a culture of shared learning and mutual support.

Conclusion

For teachers, it is important to know the basics of computational thinking, including what it is and what it isn't and why it is critical to incorporate in the early learning setting. The application of CT in preschool brings a wealth of opportunities for teachers to scaffold learning with each child. Learning to recognize the naturally occurring opportunities for children to use these skills during everyday routines and learning experiences is a key first step. As you encourage children to solve problems with these skills, it forges a path for growth across developmental domains. Moving forward, this book will dive deeper into CT and examine how to develop these skills in young children.

CHAPTER 2

A Closer Look at Computational Thinking Skills

Thought Questions

- **How do you already encourage children to engage their computational thinking skills?**
- **How do these skills interconnect with each other?**
- **What are some new ways you might promote children's computational thinking skills?**

Computational thinking does not develop in isolation. It involves various analytical skills and requires continuous practice and application. In early childhood, it is important for children to practice the four major CT skills—decomposition, pattern recognition, abstraction, and algorithmic thinking—in their daily lives because it helps build strong thinking habits and processes. When children possess a solid foundation in CT, it means they have not only practiced the major CT skills but have also developed the mindset that allows them to approach problems systematically, creatively, and effectively. In turn, applying CT skills in real-life situations reinforces this mindset. Over time, this practice refines their CT skills and helps them approach increasingly complex tasks with confidence. This cyclical relationship between possessing and applying CT skills illustrates how computational thinking is an ongoing process. Each new experience with CT allows children to deepen their thinking and transfer these skills to broader and more abstract contexts.

There are many learning experiences, activities, and routines in which children already regularly engage in the early learning setting that require and further nurture their CT skills. (This is explored further in Chapter 3.) For example, when children sort play materials during cleanup time, they are actively using CT skills. One skill, decomposition, is involved because children are breaking down a larger task—organizing the play materials—into smaller, more manageable parts. They first decide on organizational categories such as type (e.g., cars, dolls, blocks) or color. By sorting these play materials into the right categories, they can then place them in the right spots (e.g., books on the shelf in the literacy learning center, paintbrushes in containers in the art learning center). Instead of cleaning up everything at once, classifying attributes to decompose the task makes it easier for children to approach and complete.

Additionally, pattern recognition—another major CT skill—comes into play during cleanup time as children identify the patterns of play materials' attributes to complete the task successfully. For instance, children may notice that blocks of a certain size or shape fit more neatly together in a specific bin or that grouping crayons and markers by color and arranging them in the sequence of the rainbow makes them easier to find the next time they are needed. When children notice and practice patterns by repeating, creating, or extending them, they begin to recognize the relationships and structures in their environment. These activities help children see how patterns can simplify tasks, enhance organization, and reveal logical systems.

By practicing these skills and the techniques they entail with tasks that are familiar and performed frequently, as children grow, they gradually develop the ability to apply this structured approach to more complex tasks, such as organizing information, planning projects, and solving multifaceted problems (Bers 2021). Such experiences provide children with the groundwork for using these attributes as data in problem solving and decision making in their future lives—a key component of CT.

This chapter begins with an exploration of how computational thinking relates to the cognitive and social and emotional domains of children's development. It then overviews the four major computational skills in greater detail, digging into the key concepts that underlie each skill as well as how the major CT skills overlap with one another. As part of this discussion, the chapter also touches on teacher intervention during CT learning experiences, including knowing when to get involved and how to use questions to support and extend children's CT skills.

Understanding Connections to the Cognitive and Social and Emotional Domains

As noted in the previous chapter, CT is widely recognized as a crucial twenty-first century skill (Partnership for 21st Century Skills 2009). To hone this ability and become an effective, resilient, and creative problem solver, it is critical to develop from an early age the thinking and learning processes as well as the positive and proactive mindset necessary to approach and resolve challenges (Barr & Stephenson 2011; ISTE & CSTA 2011; Zeng, Yang, & Bautista 2023). This involves skills that fall under two different but interconnected developmental domains, the cognitive and the social and emotional.

The cognitive domain refers to the growth and change in a child's intellectual abilities, their brain development, and their capacity to understand and learn about the world. Its processes provide the tools needed to identify, analyze, and solve problems. Meanwhile, the social and emotional domain focuses on a child's ability to understand and regulate emotions, form positive relationships, and engage in behaviors like perseverance, curiosity, and a proactive approach to challenges. This domain is closely aligned with what educational psychology refers to as the affective domain. While the affective domain emphasizes an individual's emotional responses and attitudinal dispositions, the social and emotional domain broadens to include interpersonal skills and the ability to navigate social interactions effectively (CASEL, n.d.). These capacities not only motivate children to persist through difficulties, they also create the foundation for effective problem solving.

> While problem solving, the cognitive and social and emotional domains work hand in hand. Knowing what to do when a problem arises significantly impacts a child's disposition toward that problem.

While problem solving, the cognitive and social and emotional domains work hand in hand. Knowing what to do when a problem arises significantly impacts a child's disposition toward that problem. When faced with challenging tasks, young children often experience and express frustration and may be tempted to give up. This is normal behavior in early childhood (Joseph & Strain 2003). That said, when a child knows how to approach a problem, they are less likely to feel overwhelmed by challenges. In other words, cognitive skills influence how a child feels about, perceives, and tackles a complex problem. For example, when children start building with blocks, they may initially struggle to create a stable structure. Over time, they experiment with different strategies and discover patterns, such as making the base of a structure wider for a sturdier foundation. Through this process, they develop problem-solving skills that help them approach building structures and similar tasks more confidently and methodically. This reduces frustration and fosters a sense of accomplishment and a positive attitude toward tackling challenges. Conversely, when children lack these strategic skills, they may find the task too difficult, become frustrated, and avoid engaging in similar challenges in the future.

Moreover, a child's disposition toward problems directly affects their thinking skills. If children easily become frustrated and give up when faced with a challenge, their thinking skills are less likely to develop since they have fewer opportunities to practice them. As a result, their cognitive abilities associated with CT will be less advanced. For instance, if children have a negative attitude toward tackling problems, they are less likely to persist and may leave tasks unfinished. However, with a positive mindset, children are more likely to try different approaches when their initial strategy doesn't work, such as rearranging blocks to achieve better balance or talking with peers about how to make the structure stronger. This mindset encourages persistence and creative problem solving, helping children develop their thinking skills through challenging problems. With this attitude, children feel less anxious about difficult tasks and find more joy in creatively seeking solutions.

Computational Thinking Skills

By supporting CT skills, teachers prepare children to become more competent and effective problem solvers, equipping them not only for careers in technology but also for a future where they can leverage these thinking skills in various fields. To facilitate children's CT development, it is essential to understand which skills are involved and how to help children practice them.

BOX 2.1

Tips for Nurturing a Positive Mindset in Children

Providing children with encouraging feedback and a supportive learning setting is important in helping them develop a positive mindset toward problem solving. This means creating an environment where children feel that their efforts are seen and valued. It is also a place where they do not fear mistakes or failure. Children need to feel that if something doesn't work, it is always okay to try another method to fix the problem.

Here are some practical ideas and strategies to keep in mind when offering feedback and cultivating the learning environment:

- **Focus on effort instead of outcome.** Rather than commenting on the end result, highlight something about the child's process to get there (e.g., "I noticed how you tried different ways to rotate and fit those puzzle pieces. That's great problem solving!").
- **Celebrate mistakes as learning opportunities.** Reinforce the idea that making mistakes and exploring how to fix them are natural parts of learning (e.g., "It's okay that the ramp you built fell over. Let's figure out how to make it sturdy enough to hold the ball next time").
- **Be specific.** Instead of general, vague praise like "Good job," provide specific feedback that acknowledges the individual child's strategies (e.g., "You did a great job noticing that putting the bigger blocks at the bottom keeps your tower stable").
- **Model a growth mindset.** Share stories about your own problem-solving efforts—including mistakes!—to show that learning is an ongoing process (e.g., "When the two sides of my balance scale were not equal, I tried slowly adding more marbles to the higher plate until it was level with the other plate").
- **Encourage collaboration.** Create opportunities for children to work together on challenges. Peer discussions often provide fresh perspectives, build confidence, and foster teamwork (e.g., "Everyone is going to have a partner for this next one! Work together to locate all the objects on the scavenger hunt list").
- **Provide open-ended challenges.** Offer learning experiences that allow for multiple solutions and emphasize exploration (e.g., "How can you build a bridge that doesn't fall down?").

Many organizations and researchers have worked to identify and define CT skills. The International Society for Technology in Education (ISTE) and the Computer Science Teachers Association (CSTA), two leading organizations in technology and computer science education that strongly advocate for the integration of CT across all levels of education, developed a widely accepted framework with support from the National Science Foundation. The framework was built through a rigorous process that included thorough literature reviews, surveys of STEM educators, and review and input from experts as well as the public. It highlights core CT skills, which include but are not limited to the following (ISTE & CSTA 2011):

- **Formulating problems,** which involves transforming real-world problems in a way that can be solved using computational tools and techniques. It requires identifying and defining the problem clearly.
- **Logically organizing and analyzing data,** which includes sorting, organizing, and examining data in a coherent manner to draw meaningful conclusions. It involves understanding patterns, trends, and relationships within the data.
- **Representing data through abstractions,** which involves creating models or simulations to represent data and processes. Abstractions help in managing complexity by focusing on the essential features of a problem while ignoring unnecessary details.
- **Automating solutions through algorithmic thinking,** which focuses on developing step-by-step procedures (algorithms) to solve problems. It includes designing, implementing, and testing these algorithms to ensure they work correctly.
- **Identifying, analyzing, and implementing possible solutions,** which involves evaluating different solutions and selecting the most effective one. It also includes the iterative process of testing, debugging, and refining solutions.
- **Generalizing and transferring problem-solving processes,** or applying the problem-solving techniques learned in one context to different problems or disciplines. It helps in recognizing similarities between problems and adapting solutions accordingly.

This CT skill set is applicable for all students from kindergarten through grade 12, and it aims to provide educators with a comprehensive framework for integrating computational thinking in educational settings (ISTE & CSTA 2011). Although the framework does not specifically address the preschool level, considering the developmental continuum from preschool to kindergarten, it is essential to recognize and support foundational CT skills in younger children. By examining the framework through an early childhood education lens, educators can adapt and apply its core principles to preschool settings, helping children naturally progress into more formal CT learning in kindergarten.

With a more pronounced emphasis on the CT skill set in early childhood education, Bers (2021) conducted extensive research on children's coding, robotics, and computational thinking. Her work highlights the various skills involved in CT and their importance from a young age. Broadly describing CT as recognizing patterns in processes and troubleshooting to resolve errors, Bers (2021) presents seven ideas to explain children's CT skills: (1) algorithms; (2) modularity, or breaking down large tasks into smaller ones; (3) control structure, or recognizing patterns and understanding cause and effect; (4) representation; (5) recognition of hardware and software; (6) design process, or the cyclic nature of creative processes, including planning, creating, testing, and refining; and (7) debugging, or identifying problems and developing strategies to fix them. By emphasizing these seven powerful ideas, educators of young children can build a strong foundation in CT from early childhood.

> Four major CT skills are widely accepted and used in educational settings to explain and apply computational thinking across age groups: decomposition, pattern recognition, abstraction, and algorithmic thinking.

Based on the framework from ISTE and CSTA (2011), the findings from Bers (2021), and research from other computational thinking pioneers like Jeannette Wing (2006, 2008), four major CT skills are widely accepted and used in educational settings to explain and apply computational thinking across age groups: decomposition, pattern recognition, abstraction, and algorithmic thinking. It should be noted that in the literature on CT, some researchers may refer to additional skills or use different terms to describe similar concepts. For the purposes of this book, the focus will be on these four skills, which will be consistently referred to as named earlier. The sections that follow provide more detailed explanations of each CT skill, along with an overview of the key concepts underlying them. The key concepts are ordered from simplest to most complex as appropriate for the development progression of young children. Figure 2.1 offers a concise summary of this information.

Before delving into the individual computational thinking skills, it's important to understand that all four are inherently interconnected, often overlapping and reinforcing each other. When children engage in a learning experience that emphasizes one CT skill, they often apply several other CT skills simultaneously. Consequently, the underlying key concepts among the CT skills also overlap. For example, sequencing may play a role in both algorithmic thinking and abstraction. Understanding these points of intersection helps educators design more integrated, more holistic, and richer learning experiences that allow children to practice and develop their CT skills more effectively.

Consider when children plant seeds, a hands-on activity with the goal of helping children develop algorithmic thinking. Children follow a specific sequence of steps to plant the seeds. They might start by filling a pot with soil, making a small hole, placing the seed inside, covering it with soil, and then watering it. By following this procedure, they learn the importance of following an algorithm to achieve a desired outcome. This learning experience also involves decomposition. It can be broken down into smaller tasks, such as gathering materials, preparing the soil, placing the seed in the soil, and caring for the plant. By focusing on each task separately, children can manage and understand the process more easily. When planting a seed, children can recognize the pattern of planting or gardening and use that same pattern to plant other kinds of seeds.

In addition, as the seed sprouts and grows into a plant, children can also observe patterns in plant growth by noting changes over time, such as when the seedling emerges, when leaves appear, and how the plant continues to grow. Recognizing these patterns helps them understand the stages of plant development. This activity can also help children learn to focus on important information while ignoring unimportant details. For example, they might discover the type of soil and the amount of water they provide are crucial factors for the seed to grow, whereas the color of the pot is not. Children can then generalize this process to other plants, understanding that while the steps might be slightly different for various plants, the core process of planting and nurturing remains the same.

Figure 2.1 Key Concepts Underlying the Four Major Computational Thinking Skills

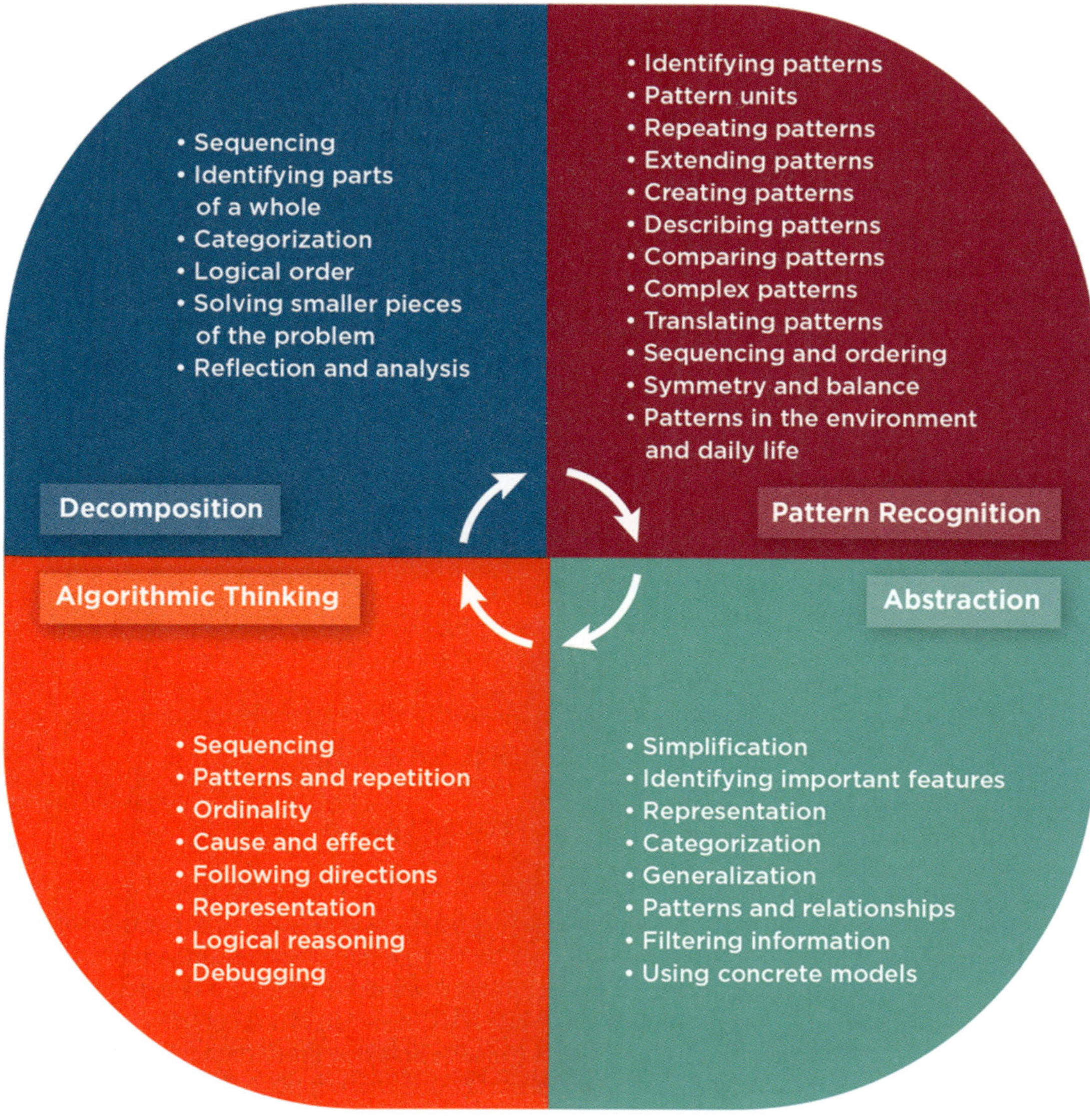

As you can see, a single learning experience in practice can encompass a range of skills, from problem solving and logical reasoning to creativity and collaboration. This multifaceted approach not only enhances computational thinking but also promotes children's cognitive and social and emotional development by engaging them with fundamental concepts appropriate for early childhood. By introducing and practicing these skills early, children advance their CT development from a young age.

Decomposition

Decomposition, also known as problem reformulation, involves breaking down complex or large tasks into smaller, more manageable parts (Wang, Shen, & Chao 2022). Often, children (and adults!) can feel overwhelmed when faced with a complex problem. By identifying and isolating the smaller components of a problem, children can address each part individually, making the overall problem and navigating the path to solving it less daunting. Decomposition also allows for a structured approach to problem solving, enabling children to focus on and understand one aspect at a time and gradually build toward a complete solution.

Key Concepts

The key concepts explored in this section are integral to teaching decomposition to preschoolers in developmentally appropriate ways.

Sequencing. Sequencing helps children understand that certain steps need to be completed before others. For instance, when breaking down the task of drawing a picture, a child may realize they need to draw the outline before adding the details or coloring it in.

Identifying parts of a whole. Helping children recognize that a whole task or object can be divided into smaller, manageable parts is essential for developing their decomposition skills. For example, when building a LEGO structure, a teacher might guide children to break the task into steps: selecting the correct LEGO pieces, deciding where each piece fits, attaching them securely, and repeating this process until the structure is complete. By breaking down the activity of building a tower into smaller actions, children learn to see how each step contributes to the final structure. This process teaches them to focus on details, follow a sequence, and understand how individual components come together to form a complete task or object.

Categorization. Teaching children to group similar tasks or objects together helps them see the relationship between different parts and how they contribute to the whole. For example, cleanup time is a perfect opportunity for children to practice categorization skills. During cleanup, children might categorize all play materials that need to be put away, grouping them by type (e.g., blocks, dolls, cars) to restore them to their places (e.g., art supplies into the right containers, books to the bookshelves).

Logical order. Encouraging children to arrange steps or parts in a logical order helps them develop reasoning skills and understand cause-and-effect relationships. While logical ordering emphasizes organizing actions in a way that makes sense, it also aligns with logical reasoning by promoting systematic information processing. For example, during snack time, children wash their hands, pick up their plates and cups, choose a snack, and sit down at the table to eat. By breaking down the routine into actionable steps, children see how each action contributes to the goal of snack time. With teacher guidance, they can also understand why this routine's steps happen in the order they do. Washing hands before touching food, for instance, helps prevent the spread of germs. Experiences like these nurture their reasoning and problem-solving skills, preparing them for more complex tasks in the future.

Solving smaller pieces of the problem. By focusing on smaller pieces of the main problem, children can tackle solving each part individually, building confidence and understanding as they work toward solving the entire problem. Having children solve smaller pieces of the problem helps them focus on manageable tasks and feel confident, and it promotes systematic thinking, making it an essential skill in computational thinking.

Reflection and analysis. Incorporate time to allow preschoolers to reflect on their actions and analyze the outcomes, helping them understand what worked and what didn't. This reflection improves their problem-solving skills and fosters self-awareness and a growth mindset, making them more confident and effective learners.

Overlap with Other Major CT Skills

Decomposition is closely connected with algorithmic thinking. Breaking down a complex task into smaller steps is essential for creating effective algorithms. When children learn to decompose tasks, they can better understand and implement algorithms by focusing on one step at a time. This approach also helps them recognize how each step fits into the larger algorithm, reinforcing the importance of following a sequence of instructions to achieve the desired outcome.

Pattern Recognition

Pattern recognition is a fundamental aspect of CT, involving observing and identifying recurring elements and regularities within problems or in the strategies used to solve them (Hsu, Chang, & Hung 2018). This skill helps children understand how sequences and patterns can be automated and used to solve complex problems efficiently. For instance, when children recognize and create repeating patterns, they are essentially practicing the major CT skills needed to understand loops in programming and computer science where similar patterns of code are executed repeatedly to achieve a desired outcome (del Olmo-Muñoz, Cózar-Gutiérrez, & González-Calero 2020). Engaging children in pattern-building activities is an effective way to improve their pattern recognition skills and foster their CT development (Bers, González-González, & Armas–Torres 2019; Lee 2020).

Recognizing patterns not only reinforces children's understanding of patterns, it also strengthens their problem-solving capacity. When children recognize patterns across multiple problems, they can apply previously successful strategies to a new context. This transfer of knowledge allows them to generalize and approach problems more confidently and efficiently. In other words, by observing commonalities, children can begin to make connections, draw conclusions, and develop a more streamlined approach to problem solving. For example, they might reuse a solution and approach used for a previous problem to resolve a new but similar problem. Through hands-on activities, children develop a foundational skill that aids in more intuitively generalizing and applying learned strategies to a variety of situations.

Key Concepts

Teaching pattern recognition to preschoolers involves introducing several key concepts that help children identify, understand, and create patterns. These concepts form the basis for mathematical thinking and problem-solving skills.

Identifying patterns. The most basic concept is recognizing and identifying patterns in children's daily lives. Children must identify a pattern before they can move forward to copy or reproduce patterns. This can include visual patterns (e.g., shapes, colors), auditory patterns (e.g., clapping, music rhythms), and physical patterns (e.g., dance steps, routines).

Pattern units. Teaching children to recognize the smallest repeating unit in a pattern helps them understand the building blocks of patterns. For example, when presented with a color pattern sequence of *red, blue, red, blue, red, blue,* it is important to help children see that the smallest unit of this pattern is *red, blue,* which is an example of an *ab* pattern.

Complex patterns. Once children are familiar with basic pattern units, they can be introduced to more complex patterns, such as *abc* or *aabb* sequences. These patterns challenge children to think more deeply and recognize more intricate sequences. For example, a teacher can create and display an *abc* pattern with red, blue, and green beads. The teacher then asks the children, "What comes next?" and encourages them to rationalize their answer by explaining how they identified the sequence (e.g., "How did you know?"). This promotes deeper cognitive processing and enhances children's ability to articulate their thought process, building a stronger understanding of more complex patterns and their underlying rules.

Repeating patterns. As noted earlier, repeating patterns are the foundation of loops that are used to execute repeated commands in computer science. Teaching children to recognize and create simple repeating patterns, such as *apple, banana* (*ab* pattern) or *circle, square, square* (*abb* pattern), helps them understand the concept of repetition and predictability. This fundamental understanding not only helps their cognitive development but also lays the groundwork for more advanced concepts in computational thinking and problem solving.

Extending patterns. Once children can identify repeating patterns, the next step is to extend them. This involves predicting what comes next in a sequence and continuing the pattern appropriately.

Creating patterns. Encouraging children to create their own patterns using various materials (e.g., blocks, beads, drawings) helps reinforce their understanding and allows them to apply the concept creatively.

Describing patterns. Teaching children to identify patterns using words helps develop their language and cognitive skills. For example, a teacher may show children a red card and a blue card alternately and then ask them what would come next. In order for children to make this kind of prediction, "pattern units must be repeated at least three times before there is enough evidence to understand a pattern's structure" (Hynes-Berry & Grandau 2019, 33). Teachers can also use clapping, body movements, stories, or songs based on children's interests to further reinforce the concept. By incorporating verbal descriptions and interactive activities, children enhance their ability to articulate and understand patterns.

Comparing patterns. Children can compare patterns to identify similarities and differences. This might involve comparing two sequences to see if they follow the same rule. For example, a teacher can create two sequences of colored blocks: one that goes *red block, blue block, red block, blue block, red block, blue block* (an *ab* pattern) and a second that goes *yellow block, green block, yellow block, green block, yellow block, green block* (another *ab* pattern). The teacher can then ask the children to compare the two patterns and identify if they follow the same rule. Another activity could involve presenting two different pattern units, such as a *red, blue* (*ab*) pattern and a *red, red, blue, blue* (*aabb*) pattern. Children can be invited to compare the patterns and explain how they are different. This activity helps children develop critical thinking skills and enhances their ability to observe and articulate the similarities and differences between patterns, fostering a deeper understanding of pattern recognition and comparison.

Translating patterns. Translating patterns involves representing a pattern in a different way. For instance, a child might create a visual pattern with colored blocks and then represent the same pattern with different materials, like stickers or drawings. This process helps children see the underlying structure of a pattern, rather than focusing on the specific objects used. Recognizing that the same pattern can be expressed in multiple ways deepens understanding, supports flexible thinking, and fosters the ability to identify patterns across different contexts.

Sequencing and ordering. Understanding that patterns are sequences helps children grasp the concept of logical progression and structure. Learning experiences that involve arranging objects or performing actions in a specific sequence reinforce this idea. For instance, teachers can invite children to follow a sequence of dance movements to the music, such as *clap, stomp, jump, clap, stomp, jump, clap, stomp, jump* (*abc* pattern). As the music plays, children perform the movements in the correct progression, helping them internalize the concept of sequencing and ordering. To support learning, the teacher may begin by demonstrating the sequence of movements slowly, ensuring that children understand each step. Once the children are familiar with the sequence, the teacher can play a lively song and encourage the children to perform the movements along with the music. To add complexity, variations in the sequence can later be introduced, such as *clap,*

clap, stomp, jump, clap, clap, stomp, jump (*aabc* pattern). This not only reinforces sequencing and ordering but also engages children physically and rhythmically, making the learning process both effective and enjoyable. Through hands-on activities, children develop a stronger understanding of sequences and order, which are fundamental concepts in pattern recognition.

Symmetry and balance. Introducing the concepts of symmetry and balance in patterns helps children understand more advanced aspects of pattern recognition. Balance in patterns refers to the distribution of elements in a way that creates visual stability and harmony. In symmetrical patterns, this often means that one side mirrors the other, creating a balanced and equal arrangement. One meaningful way to help children grasp these concepts is through an art technique known as *decalcomania*. Teachers can provide children with paper that has been folded in half and invite them to paint on one side of the fold. When finished, have them fold the paper in half again so the painted side presses against the blank side. Once they unfold the paper, children will see the mirrored images they have created, reinforcing their understanding of balance and symmetry.

Patterns in the environment and daily life. Encouraging children to find patterns in their environment (e.g., leaves, tile flooring) or daily life (e.g., days of the week, routines) helps them see the relevance of patterns in the world around them. To inspire exploration, a teacher might organize a nature walk where children look for patterns in leaves, flowers, and other plant and animal life. Together, children and the teacher can search for repetitive shapes and arrangements in different leaves or the symmetrical patterns in flower petals. Another learning experience could involve creating a daily schedule chart. The teacher facilitates a discussion with the children to illustrate how certain activities repeat each day (e.g., snack time, playtime, story time), forming a predictable pattern. By recognizing these daily patterns, children can better understand the concept of order and predictability in their routines. Through learning experiences like these, preschoolers learn to identify and appreciate patterns in both natural and structured environments, reinforcing the idea that patterns are an integral part of their surroundings. This awareness helps them apply pattern recognition skills in various contexts, enhancing their cognitive development and observational skills.

Overlap with Other Major CT Skills

Pattern recognition is closely interconnected with other CT skills when solving a problem. By recognizing patterns, children can understand, create, and follow instructions (algorithms) more effectively. Identifying a sequence as a pattern helps children understand that the steps can be repeated. For example, during a painting activity, a preschooler may notice that the process always follows a pattern: put on a smock, choose paint colors, dip the brush, paint on the paper, and wash hands when finished. Recognizing the steps of this routine as a predictable sequence helps the child carry out the activity more independently. It also supports algorithmic thinking, as the child begins to view the steps as an ordered, repeatable set of actions.

When children engage in pattern recognition, they also naturally practice abstraction by concentrating on the core pattern and filtering out extraneous information. For instance, when children learn to follow a morning routine—for example, saying hello to the teacher, putting away their backpack, and sitting on the carpet—they focus on the key steps while ignoring less relevant details, like if the teacher is standing or sitting or what color the carpet is. This skill of abstraction helps children identify existing patterns more easily and apply them to new situations, enhancing their problem-solving abilities.

Abstraction

Abstraction is recognized as the most important yet complex skill in computational thinking (Wing 2008). It involves determining what information is important to focus on and what information can be removed or ignored as irrelevant to the process of resolving a problem (Kramer 2007; Se et al. 2015; Wing 2006). This skill is crucial in CT as it helps children reduce the complexity of a problem—and therefore simplify their problem solving—by filtering out unnecessary information. It also aids in creating general solutions that can be applied to various problems by focusing on the underlying principles rather than specific details. To engage in abstraction, children must first clearly understand the task or problem at hand. Only then can they sift through the information in front of them and focus on the details that are essential to move forward.

When children are first developing abstraction, practicing with familiar tasks helps them develop this skill more quickly and effectively. For example, when preparing for lunch, children might need to remember a sequence of steps: washing their hands, finding their assigned seats, and waiting for the meal to be served. Abstraction helps them focus on these key steps without getting distracted by less important details, such as how the plates are arranged on the table. By concentrating on the essential actions needed to eat lunch, children can efficiently prepare for mealtime. This skill streamlines the process and helps children apply a similar sequence of steps in other related contexts, such as preparing for snack time.

Key Concepts

Abstraction is crucial for developing higher-order thinking skills (e.g., making connections, forming hypotheses, crafting explanations) and is foundational for later mathematical and scientific reasoning. This section explores some of the key concepts involved in teaching abstraction to preschoolers.

Simplification. Simplification helps children identify and focus on the most critical aspects of a problem or task. It's an approach that enables children to ignore less important specific details. This makes a problem less complex and, in turn, makes it easier for children to understand and re-create the solution. For example, when drawing a car, children can represent it using circles for the wheels and a rectangle for the body.

Identifying important features. Teach children to identify the most important features or characteristics of an object, concept, or story. For instance, if you present children with a photo of a group of animals and ask them to find all of the birds, they learn to focus on features that reliably distinguish birds (e.g., feathers, wings, two legs) rather than details that might vary widely or are shared by other animals (e.g., color, what they eat). By learning to identify key characteristics, children improve their ability to understand information and later categorize it, making it easier for them to comprehend and remember what they've learned. This skill is necessary in the abstraction process as it helps children distinguish what information is important for solving a problem or understanding a concept, allowing them to process and analyze information more effectively.

Representation. Introduce children to the idea of using simple symbols from daily life (e.g., arrows, stop signs) or basic representations to stand for more complex ideas. This can be explored by drawing symbols or using icons to represent objects or actions. For example, a red octagon can represent a stop sign and an arrow can indicate direction. By engaging in hands-on activities where they are required to draw or use icons to symbolize different objects or actions, children learn to convey complex ideas through simple, recognizable images. This helps children understand abstract concepts, improves their ability to communicate ideas clearly, and lays the foundation for more advanced computational thinking skills, such as coding, where symbols and icons are used to represent commands and functions.

Categorization. In learning categorization, children understand how to group objects or ideas based on common characteristics. This involves recognizing similarities and differences and understanding that objects in the same category share key features. For example, during a learning experience, children can be given a variety of toy animals and asked to sort them into groups. They might create one group for farm animals (e.g., cows, pigs, chickens) and another group for wild animals (e.g., lions, elephants, bears). Through this activity, children learn to identify and group objects based on shared characteristics, such as habitat or physical features. This concept enhances their understanding of the world around them and lays the groundwork for more complex cognitive tasks, such as organizing information, making comparisons, and developing abstraction ability.

Generalization. Encourage children to apply a general concept to various specific instances. For example, you might explain to children that the category or concept of *fruit* includes apples, bananas, and oranges because they share common features like being edible and growing from plants. A teacher can further enhance this understanding by designing learning experiences in which children categorize items based on shared attributes. For instance, during snack time, present children with a variety of fruits and ask them to explain why each is considered fruit. This helps them recognize and articulate the shared characteristics, such as being sweet, having seeds, and being an edible part of a plant. By practicing generalization, children develop the ability to see commonalities among different items and apply broader concepts to new situations, which is essential for understanding more complex ideas as they grow.

Patterns and relationships. As children learn to recognize patterns and relationships between objects or ideas, it can involve identifying shapes, colors, or sequences that share common attributes. Recognizing patterns, one of the four major CT skills, is closely related to abstraction because it requires identifying the essential features that define a pattern while ignoring details that aren't important. For example, you might present children with a *circle, square, circle, square, circle, square* pattern in which each circle and square is a different size and color. As children learn to identify the repeating attribute or unit of this sequence, they discover

that shape is the defining attribute while color and size are irrelevant. Similarly, understanding relationships, such as how certain shapes fit together or how one idea leads to another, also involves filtering out irrelevant information. This ability to focus on what matters helps children simplify and make sense of complex sets of information, an essential component of abstraction.

Filtering information. Focusing on relevant information and ignoring irrelevant details helps children concentrate on what is essential to solve a problem or understand a concept. Teachers can help children practice this concept through learning experiences like story time. For example, after reading a story, ask the children to recall the main events and characters, focusing on what was crucial to the storyline. Prompt them with questions like "Who was the main character?" and "What problem did they solve?" This encourages children to filter out less important details (e.g., minor background elements, secondary characters) to concentrate on the core aspects of the story. By practicing filtering information, children learn to identify and prioritize relevant information, which is essential for effective problem solving and comprehension. This ability to distill information to its most important elements is a foundational aspect of abstraction, helping children to simplify and manage complex information effectively.

Using concrete models. This concept involves using or creating tangible, easy-to-understand representations that capture the essential features of more complex objects or ideas, which is a fundamental part of the abstraction process. For example, teachers can show children a simple wooden toy car and lead a discussion about what features make the toy identifiable as a car (e.g., shape, number of wheels). Through learning experiences like this, children practice identifying the key elements that define the real object. As children become more comfortable with abstraction, teachers can introduce less literal representations, such as pretending a rectangular block is a phone. This helps children shift their focus from physical similarities (like a phone's screen or buttons) to more symbolic and flexible thinking. Over time, these increasingly abstract models encourage children to rely less on visual resemblance, further strengthening their abstraction skills.

Overlap with Other Major CT Skills

Abstraction is closely interconnected with other CT skills, especially algorithmic thinking. When creating and implementing algorithms, abstraction allows children to identify and prioritize the most important information, which makes problem solving more efficient. For example, when cleaning up after playtime, children can focus on the key steps—picking up toys, returning them to their proper places, and straightening the chairs—while ignoring less important details, such as the color of the storage bins or who started cleaning first. By concentrating on the necessary steps, children can more easily understand and follow the algorithm for cleanup, leading to consistent and effective execution of the task.

Algorithmic Thinking

When children encounter a problem, they need to create a solution, which means developing a detailed and sequential (step-by-step) procedure. This procedure is also known as an algorithm, which is the foundation of CT skills in problem solving (Shute, Sun, & Asbell-Clarke 2017). To develop efficient algorithms, children often engage in a trial-and-error approach, clearly defining and refining their steps through practice and feedback. They also employ a debugging process, where they identify and correct errors in their procedures, ensuring the algorithm works as intended. Additionally, their algorithms should be optimal, meaning they follow the most efficient way to achieve the desired outcome (Lee et al. 2022; Shute, Sun, & Asbell-Clarke 2017). By practicing algorithmic thinking, children learn to plan and organize their thoughts before executing a solution. This iterative process also strengthens their ability to construct precise, logical steps to systematically solve problems.

Consider children preparing to go to the playground for outdoor play, which is one of the most common daily routines in an early learning setting. Before heading out, the teacher facilitates a discussion with the children about the steps involved in going to the playground, such as the following:

1. The children line up quietly and orderly by the door, ensuring everyone is ready to go together.
2. Once lined up, the children wait for the teacher's signal to exit the building safely in a line.
3. Outside, the children gather in a designated area and patiently wait for the teacher's instructions on where to go next and/or what's new in the various play areas (e.g., sand area, climbing area, bike trails) that day.
4. After receiving directions, the children go toward the playground equipment or specific play areas they are interested in exploring, following the playground safety rules.

These steps help ensure a smooth and enjoyable outdoor playtime while also helping children practice CT skills focused on algorithms. If the lineup step is missing from the procedure, children can still go outside to play. However, it won't be efficient since children might scatter or be distracted by something else, giving rise to safety concerns. A child's initial algorithm to solve a problem might not always be the most efficient option. In these cases, encourage them to keep exploring how to find the optimal step-by-step procedure.

Key Concepts

In early childhood, teaching algorithms involves introducing and practicing several key concepts, including but not limited to those explored in this section.

Sequencing. Understanding the order of steps is fundamental to algorithms. Children learn that tasks need to be performed in a specific sequence to achieve the desired outcome. This can be taught through simple activities like arranging a series of related pictures in the correct order or following a series of steps to complete a task. For example, a teacher can provide a set of pictures depicting the steps for going to the playground (e.g., line up, exit the building, wait for directions, go to areas of interest), and children can arrange them in the correct sequence.

Patterns and repetition. Pattern recognition is categorized as one of the major CT skills, but identifying patterns and understanding repetition are also an important part of algorithmic thinking. In the context of algorithms and computer science, *looping* refers to the process of repeating a set of instructions or steps multiple times until a certain condition is met. This concept helps children understand that certain actions or sequences can be repeated predictably and systematically to achieve a desired outcome or solve a problem efficiently. When children go to the playground, they might play with a toy shovel, which they will need to put back in storage before going to the bike trail. After bike riding, they must return the bike to the parking area before moving to another activity. The routine of returning materials to their designated areas integrates a repeating pattern (looping) whenever children transition to a new activity. This repetition reinforces the concept of maintaining order and predictability through repeated actions.

Ordinality. Knowing and understanding the names and sequence of ordinal numbers (e.g., first, second, third) helps children organize and describe procedures accurately. This goes well with algorithmic thinking when creating steps. Helping children use ordinal words in their daily lives facilitates their ability to think and organize their thoughts effectively. One way to encourage ordinal words use is through modeling. For example, a teacher might say, "We are going to the playground. First, you will line up. Second, you will exit the building. Third, you will wait for my directions. Fourth, you will decide where you want to play and go to that area."

Cause and effect. Understanding that specific actions lead to specific outcomes helps children grasp the logic behind algorithms. For instance, when preparing to go out to the playground, children learn that lining up quietly (cause/action) enables them to exit the building quickly and safely (effect/outcome). Engaging in "what if" discussions also helps children consider cause-and-effect relationships (e.g., "What if there were no rules for going out to the playground?" or "What if we don't line up before going outside?"). Simple experiments or interactive discussions or activities where children predict outcomes based on their actions can further reinforce this concept. Cause and effect are closely related to the crucial concept of events in CT, helping children understand how one action leads to another (Brennan & Resnick 2012; McCormick & Hall 2022). While this is a very simple example, small and whole group discussions can further enhance children's understanding of cause and effect.

Following directions. Learning experiences that require children to follow directions highlight the importance of attending to key information. Following directions is directly associated with algorithmic thinking since directions are naturally sequential and provide a step-by-step procedure. For example, when going outside to the playground, children must follow a specific set of directions: first, line up; second, exit the building; third, wait for the teacher's instructions; and finally, move to the area where they want to play.

Representation. An algorithm is always expressed through a representation, such as verbal, written, or gestures. Introducing physical objects, symbols, or simple diagrams to further represent actions or steps can help children visualize and express their thinking. Bers (2021) emphasizes the importance of representation in developing CT as an expressive process that enables children to communicate their ideas. To achieve this, it is essential to provide various types of concrete representations (e.g., figurines, block structures) or semi-concrete representations (e.g., pictures, drawings) in forms that are appropriate for young children. Children can then become familiar with these representations and later use those forms themselves. For example, when preparing to go to the playground, teachers might use pictorial representations to show the tasks for lining up, exiting the building, waiting for directions, and moving to different play areas. Simple icons, such as a line of children for lining up and a door for exiting, can effectively represent each step. The visual aid helps children better understand and follow the sequence of actions while seeing and interpreting representations. Over time, this supports their understanding of simpler or more abstract representations (Murcia & Tang 2019).

Logical reasoning. Encouraging children to think logically about the steps needed to solve a problem helps build their algorithmic thinking skills. ISTE and CSTA (2011) highlight the importance of logical reasoning in successfully completing learning experiences that require CT, as it enables children to organize and analyze data to make decisions. Simple logic games and puzzles that require sequencing and decision making, such as arranging steps in the correct order or deciding the quickest path to reach an area, can further foster this skill. To encourage children to articulate their thinking, ask questions like "How do you think. . . ?" and use phrases like "If. . . , then . . ." (Qu & Fok 2022).

Debugging. Learning to identify and correct mistakes is an essential part of working with algorithms. In algorithmic thinking, testing and debugging often go together (Zeng, Yang, & Bautista 2023). For example, if a child is trying to fix the loose handle grip on a bike, they may try several different strategies, like using glue or wrapping it with tape. Through trial and error, they identify what methods are and are not effective. This hands-on process illustrates the essence of debugging: recognizing a problem, experimenting with solutions, and adjusting actions accordingly. During the debugging process, children practice finding errors (something wrong), troubleshooting, and changing methods or goals to solve problems (Bers et al. 2014; Sullivan & Bers 2013).

Overlap with Other Major CT Skills

Algorithmic thinking is often interconnected with other CT skills. For example, by recognizing patterns in a problem, children can (with educator guidance in many cases) apply the same problem-solving steps to similar situations. Take the example of going to the playground: children learn the pattern of lining up, exiting the building, waiting for directions, and moving to their area of interest. This pattern can then be applied to other activities, such as going on a field trip.

Breaking down a task into smaller, manageable steps is a critical aspect of creating an algorithm. When preparing to go to the playground, the overall task can be decomposed into smaller steps: first, line up; second, exit the building; third, wait for directions; and fourth, move to the chosen play area. Following this sequence or algorithm naturally involves practicing decomposition in addition to algorithmic thinking. By breaking down the task of going to the playground into these smaller steps, children can more easily understand and follow the process. Practicing decomposition in this way helps children develop the ability to approach any task systematically. It teaches them that large tasks can be made more manageable by breaking them down into smaller, more straightforward actions. This not only makes the task easier to follow but also enhances their problem-solving skills by enabling them to tackle each part of the task step by step.

When to Step Back and When to Step In

Self-directed play, exploration, and learning are essential parts of early childhood education. For teachers, honoring this approach means taking the time to intentionally watch and listen as children engage with materials, the environment, and each other. By allowing children space to have their own experiences of agency and discovery, you demonstrate your trust in children's abilities to generate ideas and overcome challenges. When children find a solution after spending time and effort, they experience a greater sense of reward and accomplishment (Joseph & Strain 2003).

If you observe children struggling with tasks in ways that cause them more frustration than productive experimentation, it is important to provide appropriate support. Even when intervening, however, it is important for teachers to guide thinking in a way that enables children to tackle problems without directly providing them with the solutions. Consider the case of Savisha that follows.

Savisha Engineers a Roller Coaster

Four-year-old Savisha is in the block center, building a roller coaster using LEGO bricks. She wants to create circular pathways for the roller coaster, but she is struggling because there are no curved LEGO pieces. After spending about five minutes trying to figure it out, Savisha still has not found a solution and looks ready to abandon her structure. Observing this, Ms. Alexsandra goes over to the block center and sits down beside Savisha.

Ms. Alexsandra: Savisha, what are you building?

Savisha: A roller coaster. But, umm, I can't make it. I can't make a roller coaster.

Ms. Alexsandra: Why not? Tell me what problems you're having.

Savisha: No circle LEGOs here. I need circles to make a roller coaster. A big circle LEGO.

Ms. Alexsandra: Hmm, that's a tricky problem. (*Pretends to put on a hat.*) Let's put on our scientist hats. How can we fix it?

Savisha: (*Shrugs.*) I don't know.

Ms. Alexsandra: That's okay. Let's think together. We don't have any circular LEGO pieces, but we do have square and rectangle ones. (*Indicates the square and rectangle LEGO bricks.*) How can we use these to make a shape like a circle?

Savisha: Umm, like a square roller coaster?

Ms. Alexsandra: Wow, that's creative thinking. I really like that idea. Tell me more. What do you do first?

Savisha: (*Shows a rectangle LEGO brick.*) I can first put these things together. (*Starts putting the LEGO bricks together and spends a couple of minutes arranging the squares and rectangles in a rectangular shape.*) Yes, now I see my roller coaster! It's a square roller coaster! (*Claps.*)

Ms. Alexsandra: Great job, Savisha! This reminds me of how scientists sometimes have to get creative with the materials they have and redesign their experiments. You're doing something just like a scientist. Sometimes, we have to think in new ways to solve problems. You did an amazing job figuring this out.

Savisha: Thank you, Ms. Alexsandra! I like to be a scientist. I'm a scientist with a scientist hat.

Ms. Alexsandra: Yes, you are! Remember, if you ever have a problem, take a deep breath, put on your scientist hat, and think about different ways to solve it. You can always find a solution!

This scenario illustrates how a teacher guides a child to practice creative thinking by providing minimal direction, facilitating more flexible and effective problem solving. Ms. Alexsandra encourages Savisha to evaluate the resources she has and scaffolds her thinking, enabling her to find her own solution by changing the design from a circular roller coaster to a square roller coaster. She employs several key computational thinking skills to guide Savisha through the problem-solving process.

First, Ms. Alexsandra helps Savisha decompose the problem into smaller, more manageable parts. Instead of focusing on the entire roller coaster, she directs Savisha's attention to the specific problem of creating a circular shape. This approach simplifies the task, making it easier for Savisha to tackle each part of the problem step by step.

Next, Ms. Alexsandra introduces pattern recognition of shapes by showing Savisha the square and rectangle LEGO bricks. She uses open-ended questions, such as "How can we fix it?" and "How can we use these to make a shape like a circle?" These questions elicit creative thinking from Savisha about how the pieces can be arranged to solve the problem. By identifying patterns in the shapes and considering how they can fit together, Savisha learns to see beyond the limitations of needing curved pieces and instead comes up with the idea of creating a square roller coaster.

Additionally, Ms. Alexsandra fosters organized thinking by guiding Savisha through a sequence of steps to solve the problem. She prompts Savisha with questions like "What do you do first?" Savisha immediately uses the term *first* as she goes on to describe her steps. Teacher modeling and using sequential words help children use the same or similar language to explain their thinking. This practice outlines a structured approach to organize thinking and information more effectively. It also helps children develop a systematic way of thinking, which is essential for solving complex problems.

By guiding children in practicing problem-solving thinking skills, teachers not only help them resolve immediate issues but also equip them with a set of thinking skills for addressing future challenges with a positive attitude. These thinking skills are closely associated with CT. This approach fosters perseverance, creativity, and confidence in children, enabling them to navigate and tackle complex problems with a constructive and optimistic mindset.

Questions as Tools to Enhance Children's Computational Thinking

Questions function as important tools to guide and redirect children, engage them in the learning experience, and scaffold higher-order thinking. When planning what kind of questions to ask to facilitate children's practice of CT skills, there are several considerations to keep in mind. The information that follows explores these considerations by grouping questions into four different categories.

Problem-solving questions that require innovative thinking help children develop the ability to generate new ideas and solutions, an essential skill in CT and beyond.

Questions That Encourage Problem Solving

Problem solving is the essence of computational thinking. It involves identifying a problem, developing possible solutions, and implementing the best potential solution for the problem. For children to practice their CT skills effectively, rich and thoughtful questions that invite problem solving are necessary. These questions should

- **Foster critical thinking.** Problem-solving questions require children to analyze a situation, identify the core problem, and break it down into manageable parts. This analytical approach is crucial for developing critical thinking skills. The evaluation of solutions inherent to the problem-solving process helps children develop the ability to assess and compare various options critically through abstraction and pattern recognition.
- **Encourage creativity.** A learning environment that welcomes taking risks, making mistakes, and coming up with multiple solutions to a problem fosters creativity. It promotes the idea that there is no correct or incorrect solution; rather, some solutions might involve a debugging process to identify and fix things that don't work. This allows children to think outside the box and explore various approaches. Problem-solving questions that require innovative thinking help children develop the ability to generate new ideas and solutions, an essential skill in CT and beyond.
- **Nurture logical reasoning.** When using questions to solve problems, it often involves following a logical sequence of steps. This process helps children develop the ability to think logically and sequentially, which is fundamental in CT. Also, understanding the cause-and-effect relationships in problem solving helps children develop logical reasoning. They learn to predict outcomes based on their actions and make informed decisions.

Preschool learning settings have various problems or challenges to solve on a daily basis. One common example is a broken play material. Instead of a teacher repairing the play material for children, this is a great opportunity for the teacher to promote children's CT by bringing it to whole or small group discussions as a problem to resolve.

Ms. Zuri Encourages Finding Solutions for Fixing a Broken Doll

Ms. Zuri: Our doll is broken. See, her arm is loose. (*Shows the doll's loose arm to the children.*) *What can we do to fix it?*

Maira: We can glue the arm back on. I can get glue from the art center.

Ms. Zuri: That's a great idea! *What else can we try?*

Hazel: We can use tape to hold it in place.

Ms. Zuri: Good thinking! *How can we make sure it doesn't come loose again?*

Augustus: How about we check it every day to see if it's not broken? And we don't pull out the arm.

Ms. Zuri's questions (e.g., "What can we do to fix it?," "What else can we try?," "How can we make sure it doesn't come loose again?") help the children practice problem solving by identifying the issue, brainstorming multiple solutions, and evaluating the best way to fix the play material. Reviewing Ms. Zuri's interactions with Maira, Hazel, and Augustus, it is evident that the teacher doesn't provide specific solutions; instead, she facilitates the children in coming up with their own solutions. This encourages creativity, critical thinking, and logical reasoning.

To further enhance this discussion, a teacher can engage children in a trial-and-error approach to implementing the solutions they propose. First, try using glue to see if the doll's arm stays in place. If this doesn't work, then try using tape to fasten the doll's arm. During the fixing process, use various questions to guide children in practicing their CT skills:

- Why do you think the arm is loose?
- What might have caused it to come off?
- How can we avoid this happening again?
- How do we fix it?
- What if this doesn't work?
- Why did (or didn't) this work?
- How else can we fix it?
- Why would this solution work better?

Through these small or whole group discussions, children learn to explore and share their problem-solving ideas and hear about other children's perspectives on how to resolve the same issue. These conversations reinforce children's ability to think flexibly and collaborate lively during problem solving.

Questions That Involve Ordinal Language

Modeling ordinal words in questions helps children use this language to organize information in a sequence, which is a crucial skill in computational thinking. Terms like *first, second, then, after,* and *finally* guide children in understanding the order of events or steps, fostering their ability to think logically and systematically. Questions that incorporate these words help

- **Develop sequencing skills.** Ordinal language helps children grasp the concept of order, enabling them to follow and describe sequences accurately. This is essential for tasks that require a step-by-step approach, such as following a recipe or building a model. In CT, algorithms are sets of instructions that need to be followed in a specific order. By using ordinal terms, children learn to execute algorithms correctly, enhancing their problem-solving abilities.
- **Enhance logical reasoning.** Questions involving ordinal words clarify the steps involved in a process, making it easier for children to understand and explain how something works. This clarity is vital for developing logical reasoning and analytical skills. When children can sequence events or actions, they can better predict outcomes and understand cause-and-effect relationships.
- **Facilitate communication.** Using ordinal terms allows children to explain their thought processes and actions clearly. This clear communication is important for collaborative work, where sharing ideas and strategies is key. Ordinal language helps children organize their thoughts, making it easier for them to articulate complex ideas and procedures.

Here, the scenario with the broken doll is revisited, but this time, Ms. Zuri's questions incorporate ordinal words.

Ms. Zuri Guides Problem Solving Using Ordinal Words

Ms. Zuri: Our doll is broken. See, her arm is loose. (*Shows the doll's loose arm to the children.*) What can we do to fix it?

Maira: We can glue the arm back on. I can get glue from the art center.

Ms. Zuri: That's a great idea! *First,* we will try using glue to fix the arm. Let's see if it stays fixed. What should we do *second* if the glue doesn't work?

Hazel: We can use tape to hold it in place.

Ms. Zuri: Good thinking! *Second,* we will try using tape if the glue doesn't hold. Now, how can we make sure it doesn't come loose again?

Augustus: How about we check it every day to see if it's not broken? And we don't pull out the arm.

Ms. Zuri: Excellent idea! Let's go over our steps. *First,* we'll try glue. *Second,* we'll use tape. *Finally,* we will check it every day to make sure it's fixed and not pull on the doll's arm when we play with her.

In this version of the discussion, Ms. Zuri still guides the children as they collaboratively brainstorm how to repair the doll, but now with the additional lens of identifying and sequencing steps to solve the problem. By using ordinal words and reflecting on their process, the children continue to develop their CT skills, especially decomposition and algorithmic thinking.

Questions That Incorporate Locational and Directional Language

Both locational words (e.g., *on, under, next to, between*) and directional words (e.g., *left, right, up, down*) help children explain their ideas or models when involving space. Though spatial reasoning has not traditionally been considered a CT skill, Clarke-Midura and colleagues (2021) emphasize its importance and include it in their CT framework. In early childhood, understanding locational and directional words is crucial for young learners because it helps them articulate spatial relationships and sequences, which are fundamental components of logical reasoning and problem solving in CT. This concept is critically important when it comes to reinforcing coding or programming concepts, which are explored in Chapter 4. Using questions that incorporate locational and directional words helps

- **Enhance spatial awareness.** Locational words help children understand and describe the relationships between objects in relation to themselves (Newcombe & Huttenlocher 2000). This understanding is critical for tasks involving spatial reasoning, such as assembling puzzles, building structures, and navigating environments. Directional words enable children to follow and give directions, enhancing their ability to navigate and manipulate spaces effectively. This knowledge is important for activities that require movement and spatial orientation, which are often associated with problem solving. For example, when playing a game that involves moving pieces on a board, children must understand and use directional words to make accurate moves. Similarly, in physical activities like obstacle courses, children use directional language to follow instructions and complete tasks, which helps them develop their spatial awareness and problem-solving abilities.
- **Describe sequences.** Using locational and directional language helps children describe the order of steps in a process, which is essential for understanding algorithms (Lee 2020; Lee et al. 2022). For example, explaining how to set a table involves using phrases like *next to* and *on top of* to describe the placement of items. These language skills allow children to follow multistep instructions accurately, fostering their ability to understand and execute complex tasks in a logical sequence.
- **Facilitate communication.** Being able to use locational and directional language allows children to explain their ideas and models clearly and accurately. This is vital for collaborative problem solving and sharing their thought processes with peers and teachers. When children can articulate where objects are placed or how they are oriented, they can more effectively communicate their reasoning and understanding of a task.

Directional words enable children to follow and give directions, enhancing their ability to navigate and manipulate spaces effectively. This knowledge is important for activities that require movement and spatial orientation, which are often associated with problem solving.

The scenario with the broken doll is returned to again as Ms. Zuri integrates locational and directional words in the discussion.

Ms. Zuri Uses Locational and Directional Words to Draw Attention to Specifics

Ms. Zuri: Our doll is broken. See, her arm is loose. (*Shows the doll's loose arm to the children.*) What can we do to fix it?

Maira: We can glue the arm back on. I can get glue from the art center.

Ms. Zuri: Great idea! First, let's put the glue on the part *where the arm is loose*. Should we put glue on the *top* or the *bottom* of the joint?

Maira: On the top.

Ms. Zuri: Okay, now let's press the arm onto the doll. Should we press it from the *left* or the *right*? (*Points left and then right while saying the corresponding words.*)

Maira: From here. (*Points to the right.*)

Ms. Zuri: Yes, it's from the *right*. (*Points to the right side.*) Good thinking! We will press it from the *right* to make sure it sticks. Where should we hold it to keep it in place? *Against the body* or *away from the body*?

Hazel: Against the body.

Ms. Zuri: That's right, we need to hold the arm firmly *against the body* to make sure it stays in place while the glue dries. If the glue doesn't work, what should we do next?

Hazel: We can use tape to hold it in place.

Ms. Zuri: Good idea! Should we wrap the tape *around* the arm and the body from *left to right*? (*Points from the left side to the right side.*)

Augustus: From here to here. (*Points from left to right.*)

Ms. Zuri: Perfect! From *left to right*. (*Points from left to right.*) We will wrap the tape from *left to right* to keep the arm tight *against* the body. Now, where should we keep the doll while the glue dries?

Augustus: On the table.

Ms. Zuri: Yes, let's place the doll *on the table* so it can dry flat and make sure it doesn't move.

Through this process, children learn to describe sequencing actions specifically and accurately using locational words such as *top, bottom, left,* and *right*. This practice provides a foundational understanding of spatial relationships. By understanding how objects relate to one another in space, children are better equipped to analyze and organize information systematically. This, in turn, enables them to create more accurate and detailed and effective algorithms.

Questions That Encourage Children's Expression of Thought

CT not only involves the thinking process but communication of that thinking (Brennan & Resnick 2012). Questions that foster articulation of thought help children understand how to structure and share their thinking process and additional information in ways other people can understand. Children express their thinking through

- **Oral language.** When children explain their thought process aloud, it helps them organize their thoughts and make meaningful connections (Vygotsky 1986). Verbalizing steps and reasoning enhances their understanding and ability to communicate complex ideas that focus only on relevant information. This, in turn, helps children practice abstraction and algorithmic thinking. In addition, engaging in conversations with peers and teachers allows children to refine their ideas through feedback and discussion. This interactive dialogue fosters deeper understanding and collaborative problem solving.
- **Gestures and facial expressions.** Children often use their hands, face, and body to show what they are thinking or feeling. These nonverbal cues can convey understanding, confusion, excitement, or other emotions related to their thinking. Gestures and facial expressions give teachers insight into what children are thinking and can guide teachers in offering appropriate support (Chi 2000; Goldin-Meadow 2005). Using gestures while explaining concepts can also help children understand a concept or idea better, making abstract ideas more concrete and accessible.
- **Concrete and visual representations.** Representations bridge the gap between abstract thinking and real-world applications, making complex ideas more understandable and relatable. They help children express their thinking by providing a tangible way to experiment with and explore concepts (Baroody 2017; Kolodner, Gray, & Fasse 2003). Concrete manipulatives like blocks or counters allow children to test their ideas and see the immediate effects of their actions. Much in the same way, visual representations like drawings help children physically see and express their thoughts (Brooks 2009). Visual representations can illustrate sequences, patterns, and relationships clearly. Children's drawings can also serve as a record of children's thinking processes and growth, allowing children and teachers alike to reflect on their ideas and track their progress over time.

The scenario with the broken doll is circled back to one last time to see how Ms. Zuri's conversation might integrate questions prompting children to express their thinking.

Ms. Zuri Invites Children to Express Their Thoughts Through Different Forms

Ms. Zuri: Our doll is broken. See, her arm is loose. Let's think of ways we could fix it. Can anyone *draw a picture* to show how we might fix the doll's arm?

Maira: I can! (*Draws a picture with markers.*) Here is the doll and here is her arm. (*Points to different areas of the drawing while explaining.*) We could put glue here and then press them together like this. (*Presses her palms together.*)

Ms. Zuri: Thank you, Maira. Your drawing shows the doll, and you explained what we could try. Hazel, what do you think?

Hazel: (*Looks unsure and shrugs.*) What if the glue doesn't work?

Ms. Zuri: That's a good question. Sometimes we have to try more than one way. Can you think of another way?

Hazel: Um, tape?

Ms. Zuri: Nice thinking! Tape is another good idea. I wonder if we could use playdough to show this next part of the process.

Augustus: I can. (*Rolls out a large chunk of playdough to represent the doll and a separate, smaller chunk to represent the arm.*) Look! I put the arm here, and now I wrap tape like this.

Ms. Zuri: Excellent job! Maira drew a picture to explain how we could use glue, Hazel suggested trying tape, and Augustus created a playdough model to show us how using tape might work. Everyone used a different way to show their thinking.

By incorporating guiding questions that prompt the use of different forms of expression, Ms. Zuri helps the children develop a deeper understanding of the problem-solving process and enhances their CT skills. This approach also allows them to visualize, articulate, and reflect on their thinking, making abstract concepts more concrete and understandable.

Conclusion

This chapter establishes how computational thinking connects to children's cognitive and social and emotional development. It then takes a deep dive into the four major CT skills—decomposition, pattern recognition, abstraction, and algorithmic thinking—along with the underlying key concepts appropriate for early childhood education. CT skills are closely interconnected, and their key concepts often overlap. A well-designed CT learning experience involves rich intermingling of CT skills as children engage in them. While there are additional concepts beyond the ones listed in this chapter, those presented serve as the groundwork for what is involved when children participate in CT-associated learning experiences. Teachers may discover additional skills and concepts beyond those explored in this chapter. It is crucial to remain flexible in helping children practice CT skills, including those not explicitly listed here.

As a teacher, it is important to reinforce or modify learning experiences to incorporate more CT skills, ensuring a dynamic and enriching learning environment that advances children's CT development (Lee, Joswick, & Pole 2023). Continuous observation of children while they participate in various daily routines and learning experiences, along with analyzing their demonstration of CT skills, will deepen your understanding of how children practice computational thinking in their daily lives. While some aspects of CT naturally emerge as children engage in everyday activities, these skills don't always develop to their full potential without guidance. Guidance can come in the form of intentional teacher intervention, such as conversation and questions. By thoughtfully incorporating CT into classroom interactions and discussions, teachers create a richer, more supportive environment that helps children build stronger foundations in computational thinking. Subsequent chapters will explore specific strategies for integrating CT more deliberately into teaching practices.

CHAPTER 3

Unplugged Learning Experiences

Thought Questions

- How can you help children practice computational thinking in your early learning setting?
- What existing learning experiences would you consider modifying to better support children's computational thinking development?
- What factors do you consider when planning learning experiences to promote children's computational thinking?

Chapter 1 debunked the myth that promoting children's computational thinking requires high-tech gadgets or software. Additionally, it is well established in the field of early childhood education that young children learn best through concrete experiences and interactions with physical objects (Piaget 1952). By leveraging these two understandings, teachers recognize how unplugged, or technology-free, learning experiences that are hands-on and practical naturally align with children's developmental and learning trajectories and allow them to effectively construct knowledge.

This chapter explores two ways teachers can incorporate unplugged learning experiences that support CT. The first is to modify experiences and tasks that are already part of the curriculum and your early learning setting. Existing routines, familiar activities, and comfortable environments can inherently provide children with opportunities to practice decomposition, pattern recognition, abstraction, and algorithmic thinking. With intentional modifications by the teacher, these natural CT opportunities can become more frequent and robust. The second is to introduce new learning experiences that specifically target children's CT skills. A range of examples for each method is explored in detail.

With either approach, there are some shared aspects to consider:

- Integrating CT elements into daily routines makes children's CT development more meaningful and authentic (Bers 2021).
- Play-based learning (e.g., center activities, games) makes practicing CT skills more engaging and enjoyable for children (Lee, Joswick, & Pole 2023).
- Creating opportunities for children to solve simple problems from their daily lives allows children to practice their CT skills in authentic and familiar contexts (Resnick & Rosenbaum 2013).

BOX 3.1

Unplugged Versus Plugged

Unplugged learning experiences involve tangible materials that children can manipulate with their hands, while *plugged* learning experiences involve technology like computers or digital devices. This chapter, as well as most of this book, emphasizes unplugged learning experiences because they are the most effective teaching and learning approach for children ages 3 to 5. That said, plugged experiences are not wholly inappropriate in the preschool learning setting. Incorporating some developmentally appropriate technology adds excitement as children practice their CT skills. If done selectively and intentionally, plugged learning experiences can offer valuable extension opportunities for preschoolers. Chapter 4 highlights a couple ways plugged experiences can be integrated.

- Curating and providing play and learning materials that promote CT can inspire exploration, experimentation, and creativity (Bers 2021).
- Inviting collaboration refines children's CT development because it encourages children to express their thinking process while giving and receiving peer feedback. This helps children to organize information, solve problems cooperatively, clarify ideas, and articulate problems and solutions (Barron 2000; Brennan & Resnick 2012; Sullivan & Bers 2013).

By highlighting and embedding CT in unplugged learning experiences, children are given opportunities to develop and practice these skills (Bers 2021; Ottenbreit-Leftwich & Yadav 2021). When viewed through the right lens, almost any moment in the early learning setting can be transformed into a CT learning opportunity. The ultimate goal is for teachers to use this selection of ideas and strategies as a starting point that will inspire them to incorporate CT skills in learning experiences that resonate with their classroom and the interests, strengths, and needs of the children they teach.

Daily Routines

Daily routines provide children with a secure feeling, allowing them to know what to expect (Hemmeter, Ostrosky, & Fox 2006). They help children see the sequence of the day's events based on a schedule. Children who engage in structured daily routines demonstrate better task management and self-regulation skills compared to those with less structured routines (Lee 2020). In addition, children exposed to daily routines are found to be more adept at transitioning between activities and exhibit higher levels of independence.

Daily routines can also support the development of computational thinking. Consider, for example, 4-year-old Angelica's morning routine through the lens of CT skills. It consists of several major steps (an algorithm) that can be broken down (decomposed) into four pieces: arrival, greeting the teacher, putting her backpack in her cubby, and checking out the learning centers. Focusing on even one step, you can see a variety of CT skills at play. Take a closer look at the third step of her routine. When Angelica stores away her backpack, she identifies where to put it by recognizing the pattern of her cubby space through its consistent location and visual cues like her name tag. If her cubby were to be changed in some way—perhaps if a different hook was installed or it was moved to another part of the room—abstraction would help Angelica generalize the process of putting her backpack away to its core idea: find the designated space and store her backpack.

Within this same step, Angelica also continues to practice decomposition and algorithmic thinking as she breaks the activity into manageable parts to accomplish smaller tasks. This includes walking toward the cubby, taking off her backpack, holding it up, and hanging it on the hook. Each of these steps can be further broken down, in turn, into yet another step-by-step procedure. The process of taking off her backpack involves holding the backpack with her left hand on the left shoulder strap and her right hand on the right shoulder strap, sliding the shoulder straps down her arms and off her wrists, removing one hand from one strap, and then removing the other hand from the other strap.

As this example shows, children naturally engage in CT as they move through their routines. When teachers facilitate short talks or discussion questions, children are invited to analyze the routines they engage in more logically. During the morning routine, teachers may use questions or prompts to help children structure their thinking. The following is a common morning greeting routine in a preschool setting in which the teacher, Mr. Miyazaki, integrates a reasoning prompt that involves a cause-and-effect concept.

A Morning Greeting Between Mr. Miyazaki and Angelica

Mr. Miyazaki: Good morning, Angelica!

Angelica: Good morning, Mr. Miyazaki!

Mr. Miyazaki: How are you?

Angelica: Good!

Mr. Miyazaki: Tell me what is making you feel good.

The prompt Mr. Miyazaki uses ("Tell me what is making you feel good") guides Angelica to logically think about her own feelings. Angelica may have responded "good" out of habit, but when asked to consider the cause of this feeling, she needs to contemplate what exactly is making her feel good in order to answer. This is a question that Angelica may not think of often on her own. It also requires her to engage with the important CT skills involving cause and effect—in other words, what (the cause) is leading to her happiness (effect). It may not be possible for educators to have exchanges like this with every child since mornings are such a busy time for greeting children and their families. However, when you find a chance to ask, this question functions as a tool to promote children's CT. (See Chapter 2 for more about using questions to enhance CT.) This question can also be integrated during the morning whole group time while asking how the children are.

Morning Circle or Whole Group Time

Morning routines set the tone for the day. When they are consistent and purposeful, they help improve the cognitive development and school readiness of preschoolers (Lee, Joswick, & Pole 2023). Morning routines can also be enriched with CT development by incorporating learning experiences that stimulate children's minds as they start their day. With intentional planning, early childhood educators can observe and scaffold various moments to promote children's CT more effectively. (Lee, Joswick, & Pole 2023).

> With intentional planning, early childhood educators can observe and scaffold various moments to promote children's CT more effectively.

One common morning routine for preschoolers is morning circle time or whole group time. During circle time, events like overviewing the daily schedule, introducing new materials and learning experiences at centers, and reminding children of the rules help children understand both what to expect throughout the day and what they are expected to do (Vanover 2020). Additionally, discussing the day's activities and encouraging children to predict what comes next helps them feel secure by avoiding the uncertainty of events.

During morning circle time, teachers also ask children questions like how they are doing and what they did at home or the previous day in the learning setting. When asking children how they are, follow-up questions (e.g., what makes them feel a particular way) act as entry points to encourage computational thinking. Additionally, asking children questions about what they did and why helps them think about the sequence of events they performed or experienced and their reasoning.

When children describe a series of actions or events, encourage them to use ordinal words (e.g., *first, second, third, next*) and model this language when responding. As discussed in Chapter 2, using ordinal words helps children organize information more effectively and builds a foundation for their sequential and algorithmic thinking, along with other CT skills and concepts. You can see an example of this in the following vignette.

Morning Circle Time with Ms. Hernandez

Ms. Hernandez: Good morning!

All children: Good morning, Miss Hernandez!

Ms. Hernandez: How are you, everyone?

All children: Fine.

Ms. Hernandez: (*Smiles.*) I see many bright faces. Does anyone want to share why you feel fine today?

Liam: (*Raises his hand.*) Me!

Ms. Hernandez: Liam, what makes you feel fine?

Liam: I went to the park with my mom yesterday!

Ms. Hernandez: That sounds fun, Liam! Can you tell us more about it? What did you do *first* when you got to the park?

Liam: First, we went on the swings.

Ms. Hernandez: And what did you do *after* the swings?

Liam: We played in the sandbox.

Ms. Hernandez: It sounds like you had a busy day! Let's think about the steps you took. *First,* you went on the swings. *Second,* you played in the sandbox. What did you do *after* that?

Liam: We had a picnic.

Ms. Hernandez: That's great, Liam! You followed a *sequence of events:* swings, sandbox, then picnic. Thank you for sharing! Who else would like to share their sequence of events?

Emily: (*Raises her hand.*) I baked cookies with my grandma!

Ms. Hernandez: Wonderful, Emily! Can you tell us the steps you followed to bake the cookies?

Emily: First, we mixed the ingredients. Then, we put them on a tray. After that, we baked them in the oven.

Ms. Hernandez: Fantastic! You followed a clear sequence: mixing ingredients, placing them on a tray, and baking. How did you know what to do first?

Emily: Grandma read the recipe to me.

Ms. Hernandez: Recipes are like algorithms. They tell us the *steps to follow*. Great job, Emily! Does anyone else have a story to share?

Sophia: I built a tower with my blocks!

Ms. Hernandez: That sounds exciting, Sophia! What did you do *first* to build your tower?

Sophia: First, I picked the big blocks for the bottom. Then, I put smaller blocks on top.

Ms. Hernandez: So you used a *pattern* to build your tower, starting with the big blocks and then the smaller ones. What do you think would have happened if you didn't use the big blocks at the bottom?

Sophia: The tower would fall over.

Ms. Hernandez: That's a great observation, Sophia! Understanding the sequence and pattern helped you build a strong tower. Thank you for sharing! Now, let's all think about our morning routine. Can someone tell me what they did *after* they woke up today?

Joshua: I brushed my teeth!

Ms. Hernandez: Excellent, Joshua! What did you do *first* to brush your teeth?

Joshua: I put toothpaste on my toothbrush.

Ms. Hernandez: Great! And what did you do *next*?

Joshua: I brushed my teeth for two minutes.

Ms. Hernandez: Perfect! You followed *steps:* you put toothpaste on the brush, then brushed for two minutes. See how our routines and activities have steps and sequences? These help you remember how to do something correctly. It's all part of computational thinking. You're all doing a great job practicing these skills every day!

By integrating [ordinal] words into conversation, morning circle time can be filled with logical thinking, helping children to practice organizing and structuring information in a sequence.

Ms. Hernandez uses morning circle time as a learning experience to model and facilitate communication using ordinal words. By integrating these words into conversation, morning circle time can be filled with logical thinking, helping children to practice organizing and structuring information in a sequence. Using these ordinal words helps children practice their CT skills (Lee et al. 2022):

- **Decomposition.** Ms. Hernandez asks the children to break down their activities into smaller parts, like when Joshua describes the steps for brushing his teeth. By focusing on each part of the activity separately, children learn to simplify complex tasks, making them more manageable and understandable.
- **Pattern recognition.** When discussing Sophia's tower, Ms. Hernandez highlights the pattern used in building it, starting with the big blocks and then the smaller ones. She also encourages the children to identify similar patterns in their daily activities, enhancing their ability to recognize and predict regularities.
- **Abstraction.** Throughout the discussion, Ms. Hernandez encourages the children to focus on the essential steps of their routines while ignoring unnecessary details. This helps them generalize their experiences and apply learned concepts to new situations, such as understanding the main idea of getting ready without detailing every specific action.
- **Algorithmic thinking.** Ms. Hernandez helps the children articulate the specific steps involved in their activities. For instance, she guides Emily to describe the baking process step by step, likening it to following an algorithm. This helps the children understand the concept of a sequence of instructions to complete a task.

By carefully facilitating discussions, Ms. Hernandez promotes the development of CT skills in a natural and engaging manner during morning circle time. Providing children with good reasoning questions and positive feedback helps them develop logical thinking and better equip themselves with language skills in addition to CT skills (Lee, Joswick, & Pole 2023). This approach helps children build a strong foundation for problem solving and logical reasoning. Through simple yet intentional questions and prompts, Ms. Hernandez encourages the children to think critically about their actions and the sequence of events in their day.

When overviewing information that is text heavy or in a format unfamiliar to children, it is always recommended to share it alongside visual representations like pictures or drawings. Since children at this age are typically not yet able to read and write in a standard form, pictures provide a clear, concrete way for children to interpret and follow the schedule, enhancing their ability to predict and understand the sequence of events (NCPMI 2020). Lavigne, Orr, and Wolsky (2022) also suggest using picture cards for daily tasks for young children. This approach facilitates children's algorithmic thinking, sequencing skills, and pattern recognition.

Using a Visual Daily Schedule with Ms. Hernandez

Ms. Hernandez: Class, let's look at our schedule for today. (*Gestures to the visual daily schedule, which features a brief verbal description for each event accompanied by a related picture.*) Can anyone share what you did first when you arrived?

Joshua: I put my backpack in my cubby!

Ms. Hernandez: That's right, Joshua! *First,* you put your backpack in your cubby. The first thing all of you did was put your backpacks in your cubbies. Anyone want to share what you did second?

Chandler: Me! I came here. (*Pats the rug.*)

Ms. Hernandez: Excellent! *Second,* you came to the rug. Does anyone know what comes after our circle time? (*Points to the daily schedule.*) What's the third thing we do?

All children: (*Look at the daily schedule.*)

Ella: We go to the centers!

Ms. Hernandez: Yes, *third,* you go to the learning centers. Now, can anyone tell me what we will do after the centers? (*Shows the daily schedule.*)

Tommy: We have snack time!

Ms. Hernandez: Great job, Tommy! *First,* we put our backpacks away. *Second,* we have circle time. *Third,* we go to the learning centers. *Fourth,* we have snack time. Can anyone tell me what we do after snack time?

Lucas: Play outside?

Ms. Hernandez: Yes, exactly! After snack time, we play outside. By looking at our schedule, we can see the sequence of what we are going to do. (*Encourages prediction.*) Now, can anyone tell me what we might do after we come back from playing outside?

Ava: Maybe we will have story time?

Ms. Hernandez: Good thinking, Ava! After playing outside, we will have story time. Great job, everyone! (*Points to the daily schedule.*) Our daily routine helps us know the sequence of what we are going to do. It tells us about what comes first, second, third, fourth. . . . Does anyone know what comes next after fourth?

Ava: Five!

Ms. Hernandez: Very close. We call it *fifth.* This means it comes after the fourth thing. You're all doing a fantastic job learning and remembering our daily schedule.

In this scenario, Ms. Hernandez intentionally incorporates ordinal words to introduce the concept to children and also models how to use them. As children hear these terms, they begin to use them to organize and describe sequential events. By engaging children in discussions about their daily routines and activities and using a visual daily schedule, Ms. Hernandez supports their practice of the four major CT skills:

- **Decomposition.** When discussing their daily routines, Ms. Hernandez might help the children further break down a specific activity in their daily schedule. For example, she may guide them to decompose the task of going to the learning centers into individual actions like listening to Ms. Hernandez explain what new materials have been added to each, choosing which center to visit, and deciding what to do once there. By decomposing these steps, children begin to understand how a larger routine is made up of smaller parts.
- **Pattern recognition.** Using a visual daily schedule, children can identify and predict recurring patterns in their activities. For example, they might notice that every school day follows a similar routine, with variations for weekends or special events. Recognizing these patterns helps children see regularities in their schedules, aiding their ability to anticipate what comes next and to develop a sense of structure.
- **Abstraction.** Children also practice abstraction by focusing on the essential steps of their routines while ignoring irrelevant details. For instance, they might generalize the concept of putting their backpack in their cubby without specifying every movement of that task. This ability to abstract helps them simplify complex processes and apply learned concepts to different contexts, enhancing their problem-solving capabilities.
- **Algorithmic thinking.** Ms. Hernandez guides children to create step-by-step instructions for their daily routines, exposing children to the foundational idea of an algorithm. The children describe the exact steps they have taken since arrival and the steps they will take during the remainder of the day. By articulating these sequential events, children better understand the structure of routine while building essential skills for problem solving.

By integrating these four major CT skills into morning discussions and visual representations of the daily schedule, Ms. Hernandez provides a comprehensive approach to developing children's CT abilities.

Snack Time

Snack time is a favorite daily routine for many children. Involving children in snack preparation helps them learn about food groups, gain a better understanding of nutrition, and cultivate healthy eating habits (Morin 2024). It can also enhance their fine motor skills and understanding of measurements and fractions. Snack time is another ideal routine for helping children practice their CT skills. The entire snack time process, from washing hands to preparing food to setting up the tables, requires a lot of sequential thinking. It offers meaningful and exciting learning opportunities for young children to practice their CT skills.

Making a Fruit Salad with Ms. Smith

Ms. Smith: Good morning, class! Today we're going to make a fruit salad together. Who's excited to help?

All children: (*Chorus excitedly.*) Me!

Ms. Smith: Now, let's look at our ingredients. Does anyone know what *ingredient* means? (*Waits for children's responses and elaborates on the concept based on their answers. Points to precut apples and blueberries.*) We have apples and blueberries as our salad ingredients.

Salim: Put them into a bowl.

Ms. Smith: Exactly, Salim! Which fruit should we put in first?

Salim: Apples, and blueberries later.

Ms. Smith: I like that idea. First, we put apples in a big serving bowl, and we add blueberries second. What do we need to do next?

Ethan: Mix them together.

Ms. Smith: Right, Ethan! I'll mix them together for you this time. Now, what do we do after mixing?

Ethan: Eat them.

Ms. Smith: Good thinking, but what do we need to do before eating?

Salim: We have to put the salad into our bowls.

Ms. Smith: Yes, that's smart thinking.

Ethan: (*Loudly.*) Yes! We have to put them into our bowls.

Ms. Smith: That's right. Let's remind ourselves of the steps. (*Holds up one finger.*) First, we put apples into the big bowl. Second . . . (*Holds up two fingers, waiting for the children's response.*)

All children: Put blueberries into the bowl.

Ms. Smith: That's right. Second, we add blueberries to the bowl. Third . . . (*Holds up three fingers, waiting for the children's response.*)

All children: Mix them.

Ms. Smith: Yes. Third, we mix them. Fourth . . . (*Holds up four fingers, waiting for the children's response.*)

All children: Put them into our bowls.

Ms. Smith: Yes! Fourth, put them into your own bowls.

By engaging the children in this interactive learning experience to prepare for snack time, Ms. Smith supports their CT skill development through sequencing, understanding algorithms, and breaking down tasks into smaller steps. As this vignette shows, it is important to integrate ordinal numbers when explaining to children by showing fingers. This approach helps children understand what each ordinal number represents and encourages them to use those numbers when presenting information to others. With continuous exposure to ordinal numbers, children gradually begin to use those terms and structure and communicate information in a sequence.

Setting the Table with Ms. Smith

Ms. Smith: Now that our fruit salad is ready, let's set the table for our snack. I'm going to need some helpers. Who would like to help set the table?

All children: Me! Me! Me!

Ms. Smith: Wonderful! (*Selects two children as helpers.*) Thank you for being my helpers today. What do we do first?

Charlie: Put salad.

Jim: Put forks and napkins.

Ms. Smith: Great! Yes, let's place the bowls first. (*Points to the bowls.*) Then, we can put the napkins and forks. (*Shows the napkins and forks.*) We place the napkins second. Third, we put the forks on the napkins.

Charlie and Jim: (*Set each table for six children. Place the bowls corresponding to the number of chairs. Come back for the napkins.*)

Ms. Smith: Now, let's place the napkins. (*Shows the napkins again.*)

Charlie and Jim: (*Place the napkins corresponding to each bowl, then come back for the forks.*)

Ms. Smith: Now it's time for the forks. You will place the fork on the napkin. (*Demonstrates how to place a fork on the napkin.*) Not under the napkin, but on the napkin. (*Demonstrates placing a fork under the napkin.*)

Charlie and Jim: (*Giggle and walk around the tables to place a fork on each of the napkins.*)

Ms. Smith: You did a fantastic job! Now our table is ready for our delicious fruit salad.

Through setting tables, Ms. Smith facilitates a brief discussion about steps and locational words (e.g., *on, under*). This exercise helps reinforce the children's recognition of location words, which is important for communicating information accurately, and develop their computational thinking skills:

- **Decomposition.** Ms. Smith breaks down the larger task of setting the table into smaller, more manageable steps: placing the bowls, then the napkins, and finally the forks.
- **Pattern recognition.** By having the children place the utensils and dishes in the same order repeatedly, Ms. Smith helps them recognize the pattern of table setting. The consistent placement of items (e.g., bowl, napkin, fork) forms a predictable pattern. Recognizing patterns is crucial in computational thinking because it supports children in identifying regularities, which is useful in problem solving and coding.
- **Abstraction.** Ms. Smith guides the children to focus on the essential steps of setting the table, ignoring unnecessary details like the color of the utensils or the material the bowls are made of. Abstraction allows children to generalize the concept of table setting, understanding the fundamental steps without getting bogged down by extraneous details. This skill is important in CT for simplifying complex problems and finding core solutions.
- **Algorithmic thinking.** Ms. Smith clearly outlines the specific steps needed to set the table, treating it like an algorithm. She gives a clear sequence of instructions while facilitating a discussion with the children. This helps the children understand how to follow step-by-step instructions and eventually create their own sets of instructions, a fundamental part of CT and early programming.

Post-Snack Discussion and Predicting What Comes Next

Ms. Smith: Can anyone tell me what you will do after we finish eating?

Olivia: Clean up?

Ms. Smith: Yes, after eating, you will bring your empty bowl and fork to the dirty-dish container. (*Points to the container.*) What do we do with the napkins?

Olivia: Trash!

Ms. Smith: Very good! First, you eat your fruit salad. Second, you clean up your seat by bringing your bowl and fork to the container. And third, you throw your napkin in the trash. You all are great at predicting what comes next.

- **Decomposition.** Ms. Smith breaks down the cleanup process into smaller, manageable tasks for each child: eating, bringing the bowl and fork to the dirty-dish container, and throwing away the napkin. This decomposition of a larger task into smaller steps makes it easier to understand and complete the process.
- **Pattern recognition.** The repeated daily routine of cleaning up after snack time helps children recognize patterns in their activities. Identifying and understanding these patterns is crucial in computational thinking, aiding in the prediction and comprehension of regular sequences.
- **Abstraction.** By focusing on the essential steps of the cleanup process and ignoring unnecessary details, Ms. Smith helps children grasp the core actions required. This allows children to generalize the cleanup process, applying the same principles to similar tasks in the future.

- **Algorithmic thinking.** By asking the children to predict the next steps and reinforcing the order of actions, Ms. Smith promotes sequencing skills. Understanding the correct order of tasks is essential for developing logical thinking and problem-solving abilities.

By integrating these CT skills into a simple and familiar activity, Ms. Smith enables the children to practice CT skills in an enjoyable way, building a strong foundation for future computational thinking.

Cleanup Time

During cleanup time, children pick up play and learning materials and restore them to the right places by looking at their attributes, making use of skills like sorting, classifying, and organizing. By adding intentional CT elements and fun sorting criteria to the existing cleanup routine, early childhood educators can enhance children's thinking and problem-solving abilities in an engaging way. Here's a brief overview of how the process of cleaning up can be tied to the four major CT skills:

- **Decomposition.** Teachers can guide children to decompose the cleanup process with questions like "What toys do we need to clean up? Which should we start with?" When children identify specific categories of learning materials (e.g., blocks, stuffed animals, art supplies), they break down the bigger problem (cleaning up) into smaller tasks to focus on individually. By tackling each category separately, children learn to analyze and address complex tasks in smaller pieces, making for more efficient problem solving.
- **Pattern recognition.** Incorporating pattern recognition into cleanup time can enhance children's ability to identify and create patterns. For example, teachers can encourage children to sort learning materials by color or size, creating visual patterns in the storage bins. Another approach could involve asking children to alternate the placement of toys based on certain attributes, such as placing a red toy next to a blue toy repeatedly until all toys are sorted. This practice helps children recognize and replicate patterns, a fundamental skill in CT that supports their understanding of sequences and the relationships between objects.
- **Abstraction.** Children practice abstraction when they group toys based on key characteristics, such as type or function, rather than specific details like color or brand. For example, children can think about grouping all building materials together, regardless of whether they are wooden blocks or LEGO pieces. This process encourages children to identify the core attributes that define each category, promoting their ability to generalize concepts and apply abstract thinking in various contexts.
- **Algorithmic thinking.** Cleanup time can be structured to help children understand and follow algorithms. By providing a sequence of steps for putting learning materials away, children practice following a set order of operations. For instance, an algorithm for cleanup as provided by

a teacher might be as follows: "First, gather all the blocks and then place them in the bin. Next, collect all the stuffed animals and put them on the shelf. Finally, pick up all the art supplies and return them to their drawers." This structured approach helps children understand the concept of algorithms as a series of instructions to achieve a goal, reinforcing their ability to follow and create sequences in a logical manner.

Integrating CT elements into cleanup time transforms a routine activity into a valuable learning experience. By gamifying cleanup time through additional sorting criteria, problem-solving challenges, and other similar components, children engage more actively while developing CT skills and concepts like critical thinking and proficiency at organization (Bers 2021; Lee, Joswick, & Pole 2023). The following sections present a few ideas for how to leverage cleanup time to reinforce CT skills. These strategies not only make cleanup time more effective, they also reinforce important CT skills that children will use throughout their everyday lives. In most cases, adding about 10 minutes to the cleanup routine allows for the incorporation of these computational thinking elements. Teachers can modify each idea based on the needs and interests of individual children in their early learning setting.

Ready, Set, Sort!

Setup: Introduce bins or Hula Hoops that are color coded or labeled with specific criteria, such as color, shape, size (e.g., small, medium, large), texture (e.g., soft, hard, rough, smooth), or function (e.g., art making, building, dress-up).

How to play: Children sort play and learning materials into the appropriate bins or Hula-Hoops based on the given criteria. Begin with one criterion and model the instructions. For example, if color is the criterion, ask one child to place a red toy into the red bin for everyone to see. Once children have played this game many times and need more of a challenge, add complexity. Including multicolored toys, for instance, will require children to analyze proportions of color and decide which color is predominant in order to place the toy in the most appropriate bin. If using size as the criterion, you might discuss what makes something small, medium, or large—height, width, weight? All criteria can and should be explored and discussed this way.

CT skill(s) and concept(s) engaged: pattern recognition / sequencing and ordering; algorithmic thinking / following directions; abstraction / identifying important features

Material Matching

Setup: On the whiteboard or another writing surface the whole group can see, write the phrase "These two things. . . ." Underneath, write a few examples of similarities that children can identify as they analyze and pair materials before putting them away. For example, you might include ". . . are the same color," ". . . are used to make drawings," and ". . . are heavy."

How to play: Children pair two different materials that need to be cleaned up by identifying one attribute they have in common. A "match" can be based on various criteria, from appearance to function. Teachers can begin by providing instructions for the matching criteria. As children become more familiar with how the game works, invite them to determine their own reasoning for what makes a match and to share it with the group. The open-ended nature of this experience encourages children to analyze attributes between objects beyond simple sorting categories, supporting analytic thinking. For example, a child who picks up a shoe and a feather boa might explain, "These two things go together because they can both be worn," before returning them to their places in the dramatic play area.

CT skill(s) and concept(s) engaged: pattern recognition / patterns in the environment and daily life; abstraction / filtering information; algorithmic thinking / logical reasoning

Guess My Pattern

Setup: Use different types of play and learning materials to create a model pattern for the children.

How to play: Children create and extend patterns using materials that need to be cleaned up. One child begins by placing items in a specific pattern, such as alternating between stuffed animals and building blocks. The other children extend the pattern by continuing the sequence (e.g., *stuffed animal, block, stuffed animal, block*). To add complexity, encourage children to create and extend patterns that are more challenging than the usual default of *ab,* such as an *aabb* pattern (e.g., *stuffed animal, stuffed animal, block, block*) or an *abc* pattern (e.g., *stuffed animal, block, car*). After finishing the pattern, children put the materials away while maintaining the established pattern, reinforcing their understanding of order and sequence.

CT skill(s) and concept(s) engaged: pattern recognition / creating and extending patterns; decomposition / identifying parts of a whole

Cleanup Relay Race

Setup: Create a relay race with three specific cleanup tasks. Introduce bins that are labeled with text and photos of the materials that correspond to each task. Divide the children into teams of three, one child per task.

How to play: Each child on a team in the relay race has a specific task to complete before tagging the next teammate. For example, Child 1 puts away all the balls into the appropriately labeled bin; Child 2 puts away all the colored pencils into the appropriately labeled bin; and Child 3 puts away all the pretend food into the appropriately labeled bin. The race encourages them to work together and follow the sequence accurately.

CT skill(s) and concept(s) engaged: pattern recognition / sequencing and ordering; algorithmic thinking / following directions; abstraction / categorization

Learning Centers and Other Areas in the Early Learning Setting

Learning center activities are common in preschool settings, allowing children to have spaces to explore content area-specific concepts in hands-on, interactive experiences (Grimone-Hopkins & Mirtes 2024). These centers provide children with the freedom and flexibility to choose how and what to play with using the materials provided. This section presents how to purposefully modify existing learning centers to integrate CT components. While existing center learning experiences already involve a certain level of CT, enhancing the CT components requires mindfulness from teachers. Recognizing and incorporating CT learning opportunities may take practice at first, but it becomes more intuitive with time and practice.

Literacy Learning Center

Both the process of reading books and the content within books can promote children's computational thinking skills. Posting a display that overviews the steps for reading with visual representations (e.g., pictures) in the literacy learning center helps children know what to do when they read while reinforcing algorithmic thinking. For example, first select a book that seems interesting; second, find a comfy spot; third, read a book from the front cover page to the end; and fourth, place the book back on the shelf (Joswick et al. 2023). Although children might already instinctively know and follow these steps, posting a written and illustrated reminder helps reinforce their understanding and awareness of the process, enabling them to recognize what they are doing and the sequential actions it requires. Reading a book also involves decomposition, as children break the process into smaller, manageable steps: looking at the front cover page, identifying the title, going from left to right when reading lines of text, and turning the pages one at a time from right to left.

Depending on the characteristics of the book (e.g., plot, topic, language, complexity), children can engage in rich experiences that promote the practice of CT skills. It's always important to provide children with books that are appropriate for their development, interests, and cultures (Gay 2018; NAEYC 2022). If a teacher prioritizes CT development when selecting a book, it is recommended that they review the storylines and illustrations to evaluate whether the books reflect computational thinking skills or their underlying concepts (see Chapter 2). By intentionally choosing books with stories and illustrations that incorporate computational thinking, teachers can balance curriculum-based books with CT-promoting ones, helping children develop their analytical abilities through engaging narratives and visuals.

Pattern Recognition and Algorithmic Thinking

Books that involve patterns and sequential events are instrumental in helping children practice recognizing various patterns and developing algorithmic thinking. These patterns can include shapes, attributes (e.g., length, size, time), numbers, days, and story sequences. By engaging with these elements, children enhance their ability to identify and predict patterns. These books also help children observe and identify similarities and differences. Books that feature characters who follow a sequence of steps to solve a problem or achieve a goal provide children with a concrete understanding of algorithms and help them understand how each step affects another.

The following books are just a handful of examples that contain patterns of different attributes and sequential events. They provide engaging and interactive ways for children to identify, predict, and understand patterns and algorithms in various contexts, laying the foundation for more complex CT skills.

Family Tree, by Josh Pyke, illustrated by Ronojoy Ghosh

Brief book description: The growth of a tree is followed from a seed to a sapling to a tall, sturdy tree. As the tree matures, it witnesses changes in nature and in the lives of people.

A closer look at related CT skills and concepts: Through its lyrical text and vivid illustrations, the book beautifully highlights themes of continuity, the passage of time, growth, and connection. The tree serves as a consistent presence throughout the story. Children can identify patterns in the tree's development, the cyclical nature of the seasons, and the recurring role the tree plays as a gathering place for celebrations and milestones across generations. The story follows a chronological sequence, showing the tree's growth and change alongside the growth and change of the people.

Pete the Cat: I Love My White Shoes, by Eric Litwin, illustrated by James Dean

Brief book description: Pete the Cat loves his brand-new white shoes. As he strolls along, he steps in messy things like strawberries, blueberries, and mud that change the color of his shoes.

A closer look at related CT skills and concepts: The book's repetitive text and story structure guide children to recognize the pattern: Pete has shoes that are one color, he steps in something, his shoes change color, and Pete sings about how much he loves the new color of his shoes. As this same sequence repeats, children practice recalling what happened before and predicting what will happen next based on their understanding of the pattern that has been established.

The Very Hungry Caterpillar, by Eric Carle

Brief book description: When a caterpillar hatches from an egg, he is hungry. Throughout the week, he eats a variety of foods to fill his stomach.

A closer look at related CT skills and concepts: The book presents both a repeating pattern (i.e., the caterpillar finding something and then eating it) and a growing pattern (i.e., the caterpillar eating foods in larger and larger quantities—one apple, two pears, three plums). It also identifies the days on which the caterpillar eats specific food. This information helps children establish the order of the days of the week, another pattern with a set structure. As children follow the sequence of events, they can use algorithmic thinking to predict aspects of what comes next (e.g., what number of food items will be eaten, which day of the week it will be).

Abstraction and Decomposition

Books that emphasize concepts like shifting perspective, identifying specific details, and using representation foster children's abstraction and decomposition skills. For example, characters who pretend one thing is something else entirely or who tackle a challenge they are facing one step at a time show children that engaging in these computational thinking skills can be used to effectively solve a problem in relatable or familiar contents. Here are a few carefully chosen examples that let children see abstraction and decomposition in action.

Not a Box, by Antoinette Portis

Brief book description: A rabbit transforms an ordinary cardboard box into a robot, a rocket ship, and so much more using nothing but their imagination.

A closer look at related CT skills and concepts: The rabbit ignores irrelevant details, filtering out information until they are left only with the concept of a box. Simple illustrations and minimal text show how abstraction allows the rabbit to focus on essential characteristics and visualize a simple object as a representation for a variety of imaginative and complex creations. The illustrations also help children understand the relationship between parts and their whole, a fundamental concept in decomposition. This is depicted by including the outline of the box as just one part of the much more elaborate whole (e.g., the box is the body of the race car, while the steering wheel, wheels, and tailpipe are imagined to make up the whole).

Swashby and the Sea, by Beth Ferry, illustrated by Juana Martinez-Neal

Brief book description: Captain Swashby, a grumpy old man who cherishes his quiet life by the sea, finds his solitude disrupted when a lively young girl and her grandmother move in next door. Despite his attempts to maintain his distance, the sea mischievously intervenes, leading Swashby to embrace the unexpected joy of friendship and new connections.

A closer look at related CT skills and concepts: As the story progresses, Captain Swashby begins to break down the barriers he has built, both physical and emotional. His initial resistance to the neighbors gradually changes as he interacts with them in smaller, manageable steps. This reflects the CT concept of decomposition, where larger challenges are addressed by tackling smaller parts.

The Most Magnificent Thing, by Ashley Spires

Brief book description: A girl sets out to create the most magnificent thing but encounters challenges along the way. Her magnificent thing doesn't at all look or work like she imagined it would! Will she give up or will she overcome her frustration to keep trying?

A closer look at related CT skills and concepts: This book illustrates problem solving by breaking down tasks into manageable steps (decomposition) and focusing on essential features to achieve her main goal (abstraction). The girl learns to focus on the key elements that matter most to make her magnificent thing, discarding irrelevant details that do not contribute to the success of her invention. She also practices debugging by revisiting her design, identifying what didn't work, and making adjustments.

Math Learning Center

The math learning center in a preschool setting includes various materials that are inherently related to CT, including puzzles; manipulatives such as tangrams, number magnets, and counters; whiteboards with markers; and dice with game boards. By using these existing materials, early childhood educators can modify or provide additional elements to the center to support children's development of CT skills. The following materials and learning experiences highlight some opportunities to encourage CT exploration.

It should be noted that the classic wooden building blocks, also known as unit blocks, that you might envision when hearing the word *blocks* can be and frequently are incorporated within the math learning center. However, equally as often, they are housed in their very own learning center because of their versatility. For the purposes of this chapter, the block center and the CT learning opportunities it offers are discussed in their own section directly after this one.

Number Sequencing Game

How to play: Children play with number cards that feature visual representations (e.g., pictures corresponding to the numerals).

Modification to emphasize CT: Encourage children to take turns arranging number cards in ascending or descending order, turning it into a game that builds CT skills. One child puts down the number card for 3, which contains a picture of three balls. Another child places either a number card for 2 or 4 before or after it, respectively. This game continues until all the number cards from 1 through 5 are placed. To support children further, teachers can add higher numbers based on children's numeric knowledge and provide visual references, such as number anchor charts displaying numbers alongside concrete objects or visual representations (e.g., drawings or photos of objects).

Through this learning experience, children identify numerical sequences and understand relationships between numbers, such as 2 coming after 1 but before 3. While recognizing patterns in the progression of numbers, they also follow the structured rule of placing number cards in order. This activity also emphasizes abstraction. As children match numerals to their corresponding quantities of the picture representations, they learn to focus on the relationship between symbols and values rather than the specific objects presented on the cards.

CT skill(s) and concept(s) engaged: pattern recognition / sequencing and ordering; abstraction / identifying important features; algorithmic thinking / ordinality

Measurement Challenges

How to play: Children measure objects with units of measurement that are nonstandard (e.g., connecting cubes, math links, spoons, buckets, string) and standard (e.g., rulers, measuring tapes, measuring cups, balance scales).

Modification to emphasize CT: Set up challenges where children compare lengths, weights, or volumes of different objects using both nonstandard and standard measuring tools. Begin with simple, engaging tasks that prompt children to make predictions about measurements

before confirming them with measuring tools. For instance, children might start by comparing the weight of two books. Initially, they predict which book would be heavier. Later, they can use nonstandard units of measure, such as a hand balance where they use their hands to feel the weights to evaluate their prediction and confirm their results. Alternately or afterward, they may use a balance scale. This process helps children understand the concept of weight and introduces them to tools that are used to measure it. It also promotes CT by encouraging them to analyze data, make comparisons, and draw conclusions based on their observations. Similarly, when comparing the lengths around (circumferences) two round tables, children can use both standard and nonstandard units of measurement. They might use a measuring tape for an exact measurement and yarn or even their arms for an informal comparison. This learning experience can be particularly engaging as it allows children to physically interact with the objects they are measuring.

Though young children may explore using standard units of measure, they are likely to interpret the findings by treating standard units of measure like nonstandard units of measure. This means that they often rely on comparing the visual results rather than numerical values. For example, when measuring the height of two stuffed animals, they might determine which is taller by looking at and visually comparing the length of two measuring tapes rather than the indicated number of inches. This approach is perfectly fine and developmentally appropriate for preschoolers. Furthermore, it promotes CT by teaching children to break down the complex task of measuring into simpler steps by using different units and to evaluate their findings systematically.

CT skill(s) and concept(s) engaged: pattern recognition / symmetry and balance; algorithmic thinking / following directions

Designing with Tangrams

How to play: Children use tangram sets to create designs.

Modification to emphasize CT: Begin by providing templates with specific designs (e.g., geometric figures, animals, familiar objects) that guide children where to place each tangram piece. These templates break down the challenge into manageable parts, helping children focus on matching individual tangrams to specific areas within the outline. For example, a template of a cat might show the animal's general shape with sections indicating where each piece (e.g., triangle, square, parallelogram) fits. This approach encourages children to analyze the size, shape, and orientation of the tangrams as they work to complete the puzzle.

Once children become familiar with using tangrams in this way, encourage them to create their own design using all seven pieces of a tangram set. For an extra challenge, children who like a specific design they've created can trace the pieces to make their own template that can be shared with other children.

CT skill(s) and concept(s) engaged: decomposition / identifying parts of a whole; abstraction / patterns and relationships; algorithmic thinking / representation

Block Center

The block center is commonly equipped with different types of building materials, from the expected classic wooden blocks to more open-ended materials like craft sticks, pipe cleaners, and cardboard sheets and tubes. Numerous creations occur when children engage in block play. Adding appropriate props to the block center can naturally enrich the dynamics, interactions, and complexity of children's block play (Lee, Collins, & Winkelman 2015). For instance, adding paper and markers encourages children to plan their creations by drawing before they actually start to build. Here are some considerations and ideas to keep in mind when integrating other play and learning materials in this center:

- Planning tools
  - Books about structures, general construction, and engineering can spark children's curiosity, provide inspiration, and expand their understanding of building and design concepts. These books can showcase real-world examples of buildings, bridges, and other structures, encouraging children to explore different architectural styles, materials, and techniques in their block play
  - Paper and various writing and drawing implements (e.g., pencils, markers) allow children to plan their block creations beforehand, enhancing their organizational and planning skills. This process encourages children to visualize their ideas, sketch designs, and think through the structure they want to build.
  - Simple blueprints or diagrams that children can follow help them understand and execute more complex structures. They provide children with a visual guide, encouraging them to break down an elaborate structure into smaller, manageable steps.
- Thematic props
  - Photos and models of specific structures like a spaceship or a roller coaster can inspire children to create similar models and communicate about their projects. Additionally, including images of houses from different cultures enriches their experiences during block play, exposing them to diverse architectural styles and fostering cultural awareness.
  - Scenario-based props like miniature diverse people, animals, or vehicles can add narrative elements to block play, encouraging storytelling and role-playing. As children assign meaning to their block creations, they transform simple materials into buildings, roads, or habitats that are part of a complex scenario.

Teachers can guide children through structured learning experiences while still allowing for the creativity and freedom that make block play so engaging. This approach not only enriches the play experience but also lays a strong foundation for critical thinking, problem solving, and logical reasoning skills. The following learning experiences are ideas for how to better promote children's CT skills in the block center.

Follow the Blueprint

Materials: simple blueprints or diagrams of structures, various blocks and building materials

How to play: Children follow blueprints or diagrams to build a structure exactly as shown. Begin with blueprints for basic structures (e.g., a small house) and gradually introduce more complex designs (e.g., a multilevel building) as children build confidence and skills. After successfully building from provided diagrams, challenge children to design their own blueprints. They can draw a simple structure, build it, and then see if their peers can re-create it using their blueprint and the same materials. This fosters creativity, abstraction, and an understanding of the relationship between a two-dimensional plan and a three-dimensional structure.

This learning experience helps children develop algorithmic thinking as they follow a clear, step-by-step process to achieve the final design. It also enhances their ability to focus, understand spatial relationships, and recognize the importance of sequence and precision in completing a task successfully (Hanline, Milton, & Phelps 2010).

CT skill(s) and concept(s) engaged: decomposition / logical order; abstraction / identifying important features; algorithmic thinking / following directions

Bridge Building

Materials: architectural books featuring different bridges, various blocks and building materials, weights or props that weigh three pounds, paper and implements for writing and drawing

How to play: Children build a bridge sturdy enough to hold a three-pound weight. Before building, they can plan out their idea by referencing books that feature different bridge designs and then drawing a sketch of the structure. Once the bridge is built, they can test how stable it is by placing the weight or prop on top and seeing if it holds steady.

As children solve problems or tackle challenges through constructive play, iterative thinking and trial-and-error strategies are fostered as they test and refine their designs. This learning experience can be done individually or in groups. After the activity, ask questions that lead children to consider the cause-and-effect relationships in their constructions, such as what happens when certain building materials are added or removed from their bridge.

CT skill(s) and concept(s) engaged: pattern recognition / symmetry and balance; algorithmic thinking / debugging

Spaceship Construction

Materials: photographs of spaceships, various blocks and building materials, paper and implements for writing and drawing

How to play: Children study photographs of spaceships as inspiration to design and build their own spaceships. This learning experience combines creativity with structured planning as children explore different shapes and forms that could make up their spaceship. By referencing the photographs, children can analyze the components of a spaceship (e.g., body, wings, engines, antennas) and decide which to include in their design and what materials will best help them replicate or adapt those components.

CT skill(s) and concept(s) engaged: decomposition / identifying parts of a whole; pattern recognition / symmetry and balance; abstraction / representation

Science Learning Center

The science learning center organically engages children in inquiry-based learning experiences that emphasize exploration of and experimentation with various scientific concepts. These experiences incorporate step-by-step procedures during inquiry, enabling children to practice algorithmic thinking and trial-and-error approaches. Additionally, cause-and-effect exploration is an inherent part of the learning process, as children observe how their actions impact outcomes. As a result, the science learning center becomes one of the most natural settings for children to practice computational thinking.

The following learning experiences are commonly conducted in the science learning center. The modifications that are highlighted offer ways teachers can more intentionally integrate CT, enhancing children's engagement with problem solving, sequencing, and logical reasoning.

Sink or Float?

Materials: a container of water, various objects that can be placed in water without being damaged (e.g., plastic spoons, wooden blocks, rocks, coins), paper and writing and drawing implements

How to play: Ask children to predict whether an object will sink or float before testing it. Have them observe what happens when each object is placed in the water and encourage them to describe their findings.

Modification to emphasize CT: Create a step-by-step chart using text and images for children to follow. The steps might include making a prediction, testing the object, observing the result, and recording it. This chart allows children to practice algorithmic thinking while guiding their exploration systematically. By recording their findings (often through drawings), children reflect on and analyze their observations. Encourage pattern recognition by discussing why certain objects sink or float, emphasizing properties like weight, density, and material.

If predictions are incorrect, involve children in debugging by exploring why the outcome differed from their expectations, helping to refine their understanding of buoyancy and material properties.

CT skill(s) and concept(s) engaged: pattern recognition / identifying patterns; algorithmic thinking / debugging

Planting Seeds

Materials: seeds, soil, pots, watering cans, paper and writing and drawing implements, digital cameras, standard and nonstandard measuring tools

How to play: With the teacher's help as needed, children plant seeds and water them. As children care for the plants over several days or weeks, encourage them to observe and describe changes in the plant's growth. Invite them to use measuring tools, draw pictures, or take photos to document progress.

Modification to emphasize CT: Guide children in identifying plant growth patterns, such as taller stems or additional leaves appearing over time. To measure changes, children can use standard (e.g., measuring tape) or nonstandard (e.g., yarn) measuring tools to track the plant's growth. This learning experience encourages algorithmic thinking by helping children to establish a care routine, such as watering the plant at a specific time each day. Introducing a simple science journal allows children to observe, record, and reflect on their findings systematically, further supporting their critical thinking and observation skills.

CT skill(s) and concept(s) engaged: pattern recognition / identifying patterns; algorithmic thinking / following directions

Exploring Magnets

Materials: magnets, a variety of objects to experiment with (e.g., paper clips, wooden blocks, coins, fabric)

How to play: Encourage children to predict which items they think will be magnetic and to test each item using a magnet. Children can then sort the objects into two groups: magnetic and nonmagnetic.

Modification to emphasize CT: During the learning experience, discuss with the children what the objects are made of and why some stick to the magnet and some do not. If they wrongly predict whether or not an object is magnetic, help them try again to figure out why. To support children in tracking their findings, teachers can provide a simple T-chart with two column headings: magnetic and nonmagnetic. As each object is tested, it can be written beneath the correct heading. You might also include a chart with easy-to-follow steps to guide children in this process: predict if an item will stick to the magnet, test it, observe what happens, and sort it into the correct column of the T-chart. Encourage children to notice patterns to help inform their next predictions, like how most metal items stick to the magnet.

CT skill(s) and concept(s) engaged: pattern recognition / identifying patterns; algorithmic thinking / logical reasoning

Dramatic Play Center

The dramatic play center is one of the most popular places during children's self-directed or free playtime. It provides a space for children to be creative and imaginative as they participate in pretend play, which can range from acting out fantastical stories (e.g., battling a dragon) to role-playing realistic, familiar scenarios they see in their daily lives (e.g., caring for a baby). This kind of play is crucial for children's social and emotional development, language skills, and creativity (Berk & Meyers 2013), and a teacher can harness the play experiences that happen in this learning center to enhance computational thinking. By adding CT elements into the dramatic play center, children can reinforce their CT skills while still enjoying their pretend play.

Running a Restaurant

Materials: play food items, pretend kitchen tools (e.g., pots, pans, cutting boards), menus, order pads and writing materials, trays, tablecloths, plates and utensils, a toy cash register, play money

How to play: Children role-play as chefs, servers, or customers. Servers take orders, chefs prepare food based on those orders, and customers eat and pay for their meals.

Modification to emphasize CT: Whether children are playing the part of customers or restaurant workers, all processes can be broken into smaller steps. For example, teachers can provide order tickets where children role-playing as servers must follow a sequence to prepare meals (e.g., "Greet the customer, take down their order, share it with the chef, and then deliver the food to the customer"). You might also introduce a challenge where chefs prepare orders within a set time, encouraging efficiency and organization. Problem-solving scenarios can be incorporated into this play as well, such as incorrect orders or missing ingredients, requiring children to adapt their process.

CT skill(s) and concept(s) engaged: decomposition / sequencing; abstraction / representation; algorithmic thinking / debugging

Visiting the Post Office

Materials: envelopes, paper, postcards, writing implements, pretend stamps, small packages, toy mailboxes, sorting bins, mailbags for deliveries

How to play: Children role-play as postal workers or customers, dropping off mail for delivery, sorting and stamping letters, and delivering packages to different locations in the early learning setting based on address labels.

Modification to emphasize CT: To make the role play more engaging, teachers can assign addresses to different learning centers (e.g., art learning center, block center) for children to deliver the mail. By providing addresses for these areas, customers can write the addresses to direct where their mail goes. Children role-playing as postal workers can then sort letters and packages by categories such as location, size, or priority. Encourage postal workers to create a delivery route, turning the play into an algorithmic thinking challenge where they plan and follow the most efficient path to deliver mail. You can also introduce a problem-solving task by intentionally misdirecting a package's address label, such as sending crayons to the block center or blocks to the literacy center. This requires children to identify the error, analyze the situation, and correct the delivery.

CT skill(s) and concept(s) engaged: decomposition / categorization; abstraction / identifying important features; algorithmic thinking / logical reasoning

Going to the Veterinary Clinic

Materials: stuffed animals, blankets, toy medical tools (e.g., stethoscopes, thermometers, syringes, bandages), clipboards, paper, writing implements

How to play: Children role-play as pet owners or veterinarians. Pet owners bring in their sick pets so they can be seen by the veterinarian. Veterinarians perform checkups on animals, diagnose them, and treat them.

Modification to emphasize CT: To enhance this play, provide a checkup checklist outlining the steps with text and drawings (e.g., examine the animal, identify symptoms, apply treatment, and record results). You can also introduce challenges, such as diagnosing a more complex illness that requires multiple steps to treat. Encourage children to document their process by creating simple patient reports with drawings for each animal.

CT skill(s) and concept(s) engaged: decomposition / identifying parts of a whole; abstraction / representation; algorithmic thinking / following directions

Art Learning Center

In the art learning center, children spend time drawing, painting, crafting, and engaging in other learning experiences that allow them to freely express their creativity. By incorporating step-by-step instructions to create specific art pieces, children can practice CT skills, particularly focusing on algorithmic thinking and debugging skills in a fun and engaging way. Teacher facilitation ensures that structured activities are accessible and appealing, guiding children's interests and supporting their creative development.

This teacher-guided approach should be sparingly and intentionally integrated into the existing learning center. Balance between self-guided play and teacher-guided play is necessary when integrating CT components into learning experiences. Guidance through models and more detailed steps is intended to be a source of reference and inspiration rather than strict instructions. Children must be able to explore, experiment, and create based on their unique interests and ideas. This approach honors children's autonomy while still fostering skill development and engagement.

The learning experiences explored next are commonly used in a preschool setting, but adding a CT element allows children to practice computational thinking skills while enjoying the creative process. For each experience, it's important to share the steps to follow to create the artwork. Posting these steps helps children recognize the sequence or algorithm needed to create the intended final work. During the artmaking process, a teacher can also discuss what would happen if a step was missed. This invites children to think about how to correct their mistake, a version of a debugging process.

Creating a Paper Butterfly

Materials: construction paper, scissors, glue, markers, crayons, clothespins or craft sticks

How to play: Children create and design a paper butterfly by following teacher guidance.

Modification to emphasize CT: Children begin by folding the paper in half. Next, the wing shape is drawn on the folded paper and carefully cut out. When the paper is unfolded, a set of symmetrical wings is revealed. Invite children to decorate the wings however they like using markers or crayons to add patterns, colors, and details. Finally, the wings are attached to a clothespin or craft stick to serve as the butterfly's body.

While children might engage in this art creation independently, providing step-by-step instructions accompanied by drawings helps children practice algorithmic thinking. If a complete product is shown, children will naturally decompose the final design into smaller tasks to re-create it. Both forms of instruction allow children to engage with computational thinking at different levels, promoting problem solving and logical reasoning.

CT skill(s) and concept(s) engaged: decomposition / identifying parts of the whole; pattern recognition / symmetry and balance; algorithmic thinking / following directions

Designing a Life Cycle Collage

Materials: paper, scissors, glue, markers, drawn pictures or printed photographs of life cycle stages (e.g., for a chicken, an egg, a chick, and an adult chicken)

How to play: Children create a visual representation of a life cycle (or another sequence with at least three stages) by assembling a collage in the correct order.

Modification to emphasize CT: This learning experience combines science and art while naturally integrating CT skills like sequencing and logical thinking. As children engage in drawing pictures or cutting out photographs and arranging them in order, creating the correct sequence for the life cycle for a plant or animal mirrors an algorithm. For an extra challenge, teachers can encourage children to design a life cycle for something imaginary, such as a dragon or phoenix. This approach allows children to practice decomposition, sequencing, and algorithmic thinking while exploring both real and imaginative processes. To further enhance CT components, consider incorporating a gallery walk where children share their work and verbally describe both the life cycle and their creation process for the collage. Encourage the use of sequential and ordinal words, such as "First, I cut the pictures. Next, I organized them. Then, I glued them in order."

CT skill(s) and concept(s) engaged: decomposition / logical order; pattern recognition / patterns in the environment and daily life; algorithmic thinking / sequencing

Pattern Painting

Materials: paint, paper, painting implements (e.g., paintbrushes, stamps, sponges)

How to play: Children paint pictures using open-ended exploration with any colors or methods they choose. They can try out different painting tools to engage in color mixing, form textures, and create shapes while enjoying the process of painting.

Modifications to emphasize CT: Encourage children to create designs and patterns with the colors, textures, and shapes they are experimenting with. Children can develop their own algorithm to achieve the final product. To promote pattern recognition, prompt children to think about their planned pattern unit (e.g., *red, blue, red, blue*; *circle, line, circle, line*). If creating a pattern proves challenging for some children, engage in discussions where you might point out options for colors, shapes, and the sequence of the pattern. Alternately, include a clear, step-by-step procedure to help children understand the process. By following the defined steps, children practice algorithmic thinking and focus on the essential sequence without adding unnecessary steps.

CT skill(s) and concept(s) engaged: pattern recognition / creating and repeating patterns; abstraction / filtering information; algorithmic thinking / sequencing

Outdoor Play Area

Outdoor play provides an excellent opportunity for children to develop their CT skills through hands-on, physical, and interactive learning experiences. The open-ended nature of outdoor play encourages exploration, problem solving, and creativity, which are foundational to computational thinking. Activities that involve organizing gameplay, navigating space, and integrating natural objects help children practice breaking tasks into steps, following or creating sequences, and identifying and correcting mistakes. The following are some examples of outdoor play learning experiences that can be modified to enhance children's CT development. Before children engage in any of the following activities, teachers must ensure that all materials and setups are safe for young children. Soft padding should be used where necessary to prevent injuries.

Obstacle Course Challenge

Setup: Create an obstacle course using cones, ropes, tires, and other equipment appropriate and safe for young children. Design the course with different stages that children must perform in sequence.

How to play: Children navigate the obstacle course to clear the various stages (e.g., jumping over small cones, crawling through Hula-Hoops, stepping through a line of tires). Share with children that completing each stage in the correct order—not going through the stages fast—is what is important.

Modification to integrate CT: Once children have seen the course, encourage them to make a plan of action for how to approach and move through each obstacle. Teachers can guide discussions with children before the learning experience to facilitate this planning as well as after so they can reflect on what worked well or what could be improved. This encourages them to think creatively, problem solve, and adjust their strategies as needed. Once children are familiar with obstacle courses, you might involve children in planning or modifying the stages of the course, fostering ownership and creativity in the activity.

CT skill(s) and concept(s) engaged: decomposition / solving smaller pieces of the problem; algorithmic thinking / sequencing and following directions

Nature Scavenger Hunt

Setup: Prepare a list of natural items, specifically those that can be found in the immediate local environment. Be sure to have photos alongside each. The list should include similar items with a variety of characteristics (e.g., leaves of different shapes or sizes, rocks with varying textures, feathers in different shades of color). Additionally, provide clipboards, pencils, and collection bags for children.

How to play: Children explore their surroundings to find and collect items from the list. The initial focus is on gathering natural items purely for the simple joy of the process of discovery.

Modification to integrate CT skills: Once children have scavenged items, encourage them to think about how they could categorize or sequence them, such as organizing them by size, color, or texture. Through discussion, teachers can prompt children to focus on features beyond what they've initially identified and considered to inspire recategorization of items using different criteria and exploration of additional sequences.

CT skill(s) and concept(s) engaged: decomposition / categorization; pattern recognition / sequencing and ordering; abstraction / identifying important features

Building a Dog Shelter

Setup: Gather and provide some manufactured building materials, such as cardboard, playdough, and rope. To enhance engagement, you might first read aloud a children's book about a lost pet to create a more concrete and meaningful connection between the scenario and the learning experience.

How to play: Children work together to design and build a shelter big enough for a dog using the provided materials and any natural items they can find outside (e.g., sticks, leaves). To start, allow children to explore and experiment with materials in their own way.

Modification to integrate CT skills: Teachers can encourage children to plan their steps before starting to build, from selecting materials to deciding on the design of the shelter. Provide children with constraints or conditions that their structure should meet. For example, so the lost dog has somewhere safe to sleep, invite children to consider how they can secure materials together to make sure the shelter is stable. If it begins to rain, what materials will best help to create a dry place? As they build, children troubleshoot and revise their plans if the shelter doesn't meet its purpose. They also use abstraction to focus on essential features and ignore irrelevant details (e.g., the shelter's color).

CT skill(s) and concept(s) engaged: decomposition / solving smaller pieces of the problem; abstraction / identifying important features; algorithmic thinking / debugging

Targeted CT Learning Experiences

With this section, the focus transitions from integrating computational thinking into familiar routines and existing learning experiences in content area-specific centers to incorporating experiences that directly target CT skills and concepts. While the learning experiences outlined here may not be completely new to early childhood educators, they are intentionally designed and structured to put computational thinking at the forefront. They serve as standalone unplugged learning experiences that can be embedded into the classroom day as dedicated sessions. As play-based, engaging challenges, they are effective as both introductions to new CT skills and concepts and as reinforcement of skills and concepts already touched on in earlier activities.

I'm a Robot and I'm a Programmer

Setup and Introduction

Teacher's preparation. Prepare a series of simple, clear commands. These should involve familiar tasks within the learning environment to be relatable and engaging. Based on the children's ages and skill level with this experience, you can also prepare a series of multistep commands that require children to think critically as they follow a more complex sequence. Visual aids (e.g., arrows, symbols, diagrams) can also be used alongside verbal instructions to help children understand the commands more clearly.

Whole group discussion. Encourage and scaffold discussion about what programmers and robots are and what they do. Be sure to invite children to describe any theories they come up with or experiences they have had. Build on their responses to explain that a programmer creates instructions, or commands, that the robot must follow. Introduce the concepts of *input* and *output,* explaining that input refers to the commands given by the programmer and output is the robot's actions in response to those commands. Emphasize that a robot cannot move or act without input—its programming. Use simple language, such as "A robot listens to what the programmer tells it to do, and then it does exactly that."

With a shared understanding in place, introduce this role-play learning experience as a two-person game, where one child acts as the programmer and the other as the robot. Discuss the kinds of directions the programmer can give (e.g., walk forward, turn left, pick up an object), why being specific is important, and how a robot uses commands to successfully move or complete tasks. You can demonstrate by acting as a robot yourself and asking the children to give you commands, responding to them and giving feedback accordingly.

How to Play

Pair off children and assign each the role of either programmer or robot. Teachers should ensure that all children have the opportunity to experience both roles.

Children who are programmers work to create a series of commands for their robot partner to follow. Provide a few constraints or guidelines for programmers to incorporate in their instructions; for example

- Start each step by saying "Robot" and end each step by saying "End" to let the robot know clearly when the command has begun and finished.

- Each step should be simple and describe one action.
- The programmer must guide the robot in navigating at least one obstacle to reach their end destination.

Once a series of commands has been completed, programmers say them aloud one at a time to have the children role-playing as robots perform them. Through this interactive input and output exercise, children will quickly come to understand firsthand how important it is to create accurate algorithms. Errors in commands can lead to the robot arriving at the wrong destination, doing the wrong thing, or just getting stuck! At this point, debugging comes into play, with programmers revising their commands to get the robots back on track.

As children become more practiced with this learning experience, consider adding more constraints to keep it engaging and challenging. For example, prompt programmers to make their steps more complex, incorporate looping by repeating commands, involve props, or come up with a storyline or theme to explain why the robot is performing these actions (e.g., trying to reach the control panel of a spaceship to land on the moon).

CT skill(s) and concept(s) engaged: decomposition / sequencing and logical order; algorithmic thinking / following directions and debugging

See It in Action

Programming Robots with Ms. Harper

Ms. Harper: Now that we understand that a programmer gives commands and a robot follows those commands, I think we're ready to try it out. Diane, I know you were excited to be a programmer, and Matthew, you wanted to be a robot. How about you two go first?

Diane: Robot, stand up. End.

Matthew: (*Stands.*)

Diane: Robot, um, go over there. (*Points.*)

Ms. Harper: Where, Diane? It's important for the robot to know exactly where you want him to go.

Diane: Right! Robot, go to the teacher's table . . . end.

Matthew: (*Walks forward to stand next to the table.*)

Diane: Robot, touch the table. End.

Matthew: (*Touches the table and starts to walk back.*)

Ms. Harper: Wait, Matthew! You're still a robot, so you'll need to stay at the table until your programmer gives you a new command.

Matthew: (*Giggles and returns to the table.*)

Ms. Harper: Diane, do you have another command for your robot?

Diane: Robot, come back—end!

Matthew: (*Walks back to Diane.*)

Ms. Harper: Great job, Diane and Matthew! Now, for the next programmer, make sure you give accurate and detailed commands so your robot knows exactly what to do. And for the next robot, remember: don't take any action unless the programmer says so. Who wants to try next? Mica and Liz, I saw your hands up first in the programmer and robot groups, so go ahead!

Mica: Robot, stand up and look at the reading center. End.

Liz: (*Stands and turns right.*)

Mica: Robot, take three steps to the reading station. End.

Liz: (*Takes three steps, counting under her breath.*) One, two, three.

Mica: Now take five more steps!

Liz: (*Lifts a leg to move, then stops. Turns to smile at Mica and Ms. Harper.*) Beep boop.

Ms. Harper: I think the robot didn't quite understand, Mica. Think about your command. Are there any words you forgot to say?

Mica: Um . . . oh! Robot, now take five more steps. (*Jumps to emphasize the last word.*) End!

Liz: One, two, three, four, five. (*Takes five steps, stopping slightly past the reading center.*)

Mica: You went too far! (*Thinks.*) Robot, come back . . . two steps. End.

Liz: (*Takes two steps back, arriving at the reading center.*)

Ms. Harper: Wonderful! That was great listening, Liz. When you didn't hear the full command, you stayed put. And Mica, your debugging skills keep getting better. You fixed two different problems so fast!

Mystery Bag

Setup and Introduction

Teacher's preparation. Prepare several small bags to each contain one familiar object from the early learning setting. Bags should be made of thick fabric or another opaque material to prevent children from seeing inside. Choose objects that vary in texture, shape, size, and material. All objects should be safe, durable, and appropriate for preschool-age children. Examples might include toy cars, wooden blocks, soft pom-poms, or plastic spoons.

Whole group discussion. Invite children to handle various objects in the learning setting and to describe to everyone what they feel with their hands and what they hear when moving, shaking, or tapping them. Introduce the concept of using their senses to identify objects, highlighting the importance of relying on observation through some sense when another cannot be used. Bring out one of the prepared bags, share that there is something hidden inside, and explain to the children how they'll use only touch, hearing, and sometimes smell to solve what the mystery object is.

Discuss how even though no one can look inside the bag, the sensory clues they gain while handling the mystery object can be very useful. Emphasize the importance of accurately describing what they feel, hear, and smell to everyone. Together, everyone's clues add up and contribute to reasoning out what the object could be while also eliminating what it cannot be.

Teachers can illustrate this learning experience by placing their hand inside the bag and describing the object without naming it (e.g., "Hmm, this feels smooth and round. What are some objects that are smooth and round?"). Listen to children's responses and provide additional clues that either reinforce their ideas or guide them to pursue other options. This approach sets the tone for the activity and models how to use descriptive language and sensory observations to make thoughtful, logical guesses.

How to Play

Working as a whole group, children take turns reaching into the mystery bags and handling the objects to see what they feel, hear, and smell. The child holding the bag provides a clue about the object inside, such as its texture, shape, or size (e.g., "It feels soft and fluffy" or "It's long and bumpy"), while the other children guess what it might be. If no one guesses correctly, the bag is passed to the next child and the process is repeated so more clues can be shared and collected. This continues until the mystery object is correctly identified. Once the object is revealed, discuss the clues that helped identify it. Continue with various bags and objects so every child has a turn to describe and guess.

CT skill(s) and concept(s) engaged: decomposition / identifying parts of a whole; abstraction / identifying important features and filtering information; algorithmic thinking / logical reasoning

See It in Action

Using Sensory Clues with Ms. Kailani

Ms. Kailani: Now, we're going to play a fun game with mystery bags! Each bag has something inside, and your job is to guess what it is. But here's the twist—you can't look inside! You'll use your hands to touch and feel the object. Who wants to go first? Romi, would you like to try?

Romi: Yes! (*Walks up and places a hand inside the bag.*)

Ms. Kailani: What does it feel like?

Romi: It's soft and squishy. And it feels round, but not all the way round.

Ms. Kailani: Great clues, Romi! I'm going to write that down on the board. (*Writes* soft, squishy, *and* kind of round. *Draws a sketch of a rounded shape.*) Everyone, let's think about Romi's clues. What do you think the object might be?

Haeun: A ball?

Romi: No, it's not all round like a ball. One part is sort of round, and there's more that's not.

Ms. Kailani: Hmm, I think we need more clues. Haeun, why don't you come on up and see what you feel?

Haeun: (*Goes over and reaches inside the bag.*) Oh! It's furry, like my dog.

Ms. Kailani: That's an interesting clue. Let's add that to our list. (*Includes the new clue on the board.*) So our mystery object is soft and squishy. It has a round part. It's furry. Any guesses?

Lila: I think I know! But can I feel first to check?

Ms. Kailani: Of course! Getting more information before sharing a hypothesis is a very good approach. Remember, a hypothesis is our best guess about what we think will happen.

Lila: (*Jumps up and feels the object.*) Yeah. (*Nods.*) I feel two ears and two arms and two legs. I think this is a teddy bear.

Ms. Kailani: Why don't you pull it out and see if you're right?

Lila: (*Opens the bag and reveals a teddy bear.*)

Ms. Kailani: Well done! Everyone did very good work describing what they felt. Together, your clues helped solve the mystery. Let's grab the next bag and solve another.

The Fastest Way

Setup and Introduction

Teacher's preparation. Draw a square grid on the floor with either three-by-three or four-by-four dimensions, depending on the children's developmental level. (The larger the grid, the more complex.) To create the grid, you might use tape if indoors or chalk if outdoors. Write *start* in one square and *end* in another. Prepare a chart that provides space for children to record their names and the number of steps they take.

Whole group discussion. Guide a conversation about the idea that there is more than one way to get to the same destination. To illustrate this concept, the teacher might point to an object that's nearby (e.g., a projector on their right) and ask children to suggest different ways to get to it. Act out several of their ideas to demonstrate each path. For example, show that while you could walk to your left and travel around the entire classroom to reach the projector, the fastest and easiest way is to take a few steps to the right. This helps children see that multiple strategies can solve the same problem, though some strategies may be more efficient than others.

Introduce the grid you created, highlighting its start and end points. Emphasize that while there might be more than one way to go between these points, the goal is to find the shortest, most efficient path. As children explore this, encourage them to use ordinal words (e.g., *first, next, finally*) and directional words (e.g., *left, right, up/forward, down/backward*) to describe their movements as well as count the number of steps they take.

How to Play

Children take turns navigating the grid from the start to end points with the goal of finding the shortest path. Make sure children understand that they can only move one square at a time and that squares can't be skipped. As a child makes each move, prompt them to describe it aloud. Once they reach the end, have them re-create their path, this time counting the number of steps they take. After they've reached the end a second time, have each child record their name and the number of steps they took using numerals or representative drawings (e.g., five circles for five steps) on the prepared chart. When a few children have navigated the grid, facilitate a discussion for the whole group to compare how many steps each child took and to decide who found the fastest route. Teachers can then move the *start* and *end* labels to different squares on the grid for children to navigate between them next. For added complexity, grids with more dimensions (e.g., five by five, six by six) can be introduced. These bigger grids offer more pathway options and therefore more variation to refine and analyze strategies. (For ideas on incorporating a narrative element into this learning experience to enhance engagement, see Chapter 4.)

CT skill(s) and concept(s) engaged: pattern recognition / comparing patterns; algorithmic thinking / logical reasoning and debugging

See It in Action

A Pathfinding Adventure with Mrs. Alleck

Mrs. Alleck: Look at our grid on the floor. Do you see the *start* label over here and the *end* label over there?

Karla: Yes, it's a big square!

Mrs. Alleck: Exactly, Karla! Remember, the goal of the game is to find the fastest way to move from start to end. You can only move one square at a time—up, down, left, or right. Let's see who can find the shortest path. Karla, you can go first. Start here. (*Points to the appropriate square.*) Which way do you want to move first?

Karla: I'll go to the right! (*Steps onto the next square.*)

Mrs. Alleck: Good choice! What's next?

Karla: Down! (*Steps backward.*)

Mrs. Alleck: Great! Keep going until you reach the end square.

Karla: (*Finishes, then retraces her path to count her steps with Mrs. Alleck.*) One, two, three, four, five!

Mrs. Alleck: Nice work, Karla. Go ahead and record that on our chart. Monica, it's your turn. Do you think you can find a shorter way?

Monica: I think I'll go down first. (*Takes her first step.*)

Mrs. Alleck: Interesting! Keep going.

Monica: (*Reaches the end square after four steps.*) I did it with only four steps!

Mrs. Alleck: Well done, Monica! You found a faster way. While you record that, Hannah can take her turn. Hannah, can you reach the end square in less than four steps?

Hannah: I'll try! (*Carefully moves through the grid, reaching the end square. Retraces her path and counts.*) Four steps, just like Monica.

Mrs. Alleck: Amazing teamwork, everyone! Let's pause here. Monica and Hannah both took four steps to reach the end square, but they took different paths. Who can remember what exactly they did so we can compare their paths?

Secret Codes

Setup and Introduction

Teacher's preparation. Create picture cards that feature an image of an item or living thing along with a short sequence of colors beneath it (e.g., a dog with a *red, yellow, red, yellow* color sequence). Gather and provide pipe cleaners and beads in various colors that correspond to the color sequences on the cards.

Whole group discussion. Talk about the concept of a *code*. Ask children what they think codes are and encourage them to share their ideas. Build on their responses by explaining that codes are special ways of communicating using symbols to share messages; for example, humans use computer code to tell computers what to do in a language they understand. Codes can be made up from anything, symbols, letters, and even colors. Introduce the picture cards you created, highlighting the color sequence that represents the image—a sort of code. Illustrate using this code to re-create the color sequence using beads threaded onto pipe cleaners and constructing a secret message that needs to be cracked.

How to Play

Split the group into two teams: coders, who create secret messages, and code breakers, who interpret those messages. Teachers should ensure that all children have the opportunity to experience both roles.

Working individually or in small groups, coders choose a picture card and use it to create a short message that includes the word depicted on that card. However, the word is not written down; it is replaced with a blank space and accompanied by a bead pattern on a pipe cleaner, making the message a secret code. For example, if a child draws the dog card described earlier, they create a sentence about a dog, but the word *dog* is replaced by a blank space (e.g., The ________ chased a frisbee in the park). The child then replicates the *red, yellow, red, yellow* bead sequence on the bottom of the dog picture card on a pipe cleaner. Both the message, written on a slip of paper, and the bead pattern are enclosed in an envelope and delivered to the code breaker. Once they are passed the secret message, code breakers must figure out what it says. They can make guesses using context clues (e.g., "What kind of animals chase frisbees?") and then check to see if there is a picture card for what they guess. If there is such a card, they need to determine if the color sequence on the bottom of the picture card matches with the pattern of the beads also enclosed in the envelope. When they find a match, they can complete the message and ask the coder if they got it right. Teachers can facilitate collaboration by ensuring that coders create messages that are meaningful and have some context clues and code breakers provide feedback as they interpret the secret messages.

CT skill(s) and concept(s) engaged: pattern recognition / comparing patterns; abstraction / representation; algorithmic thinking / sequencing

See It in Action

Cracking the Code with Mr. Hosan

Mr. Hosan: Now that we understand what a code is, let's create a secret message using a pattern of colored beads as the code. (*Holds up a picture card.*) This card has a flower on it. Underneath, we see a color sequence: *green, blue, green, blue*. That's our code! It represents the flower. Who can re-create it using beads and a pipe cleaner?

Abra: (*Raises hand.*) Me!

Mr. Hosan: Go for it! While you make the bead pattern, can you tell us what you're doing?

Abra: Yeah. (*Threads beads.*) Green bead, then blue bead, then green bead, and then the last one is blue too.

Mr. Hosan: That's exactly right, Abra! *Green, blue, green, blue* is the code for *flower*. Next, we need to make a message about the flower. What do we know about flowers? What can our message say about it? Julian, I see you have an idea.

Julian: Flowers need water. And sun.

Mr. Hosan: What a great message. It shares good information about flowers. Maybe we can write it like this for a code breaker to solve. (*Writes on the whiteboard as he speaks.*) "The ____________ needs water and sunshine to grow."

Julian: That's good.

Mr. Hosan: Great, so we'll write this message on a piece of paper. Then, we'll put it in an envelope with our bead pattern on the pipe cleaner. And finally, we'll hand it to the code breaker. Wonderful work, everyone!

Mapping and Treasure Hunting

Setup and Introduction

Teacher's preparation. Begin by placing a small toy or object (the treasure) in a specific location to set up the treasure hunt. Initially, objects may be left out in the open (e.g., on the reading cushion in the literacy learning center) to help children familiarize themselves with the experience and build confidence in locating items. As children gain more practice, increase the challenge by hiding the objects in less visible spots.

Create a simple map of the early learning setting, including basic details like the locations of major learning centers or easily recognizable features or landmarks (e.g., the front door, windows). Also put together a short list of directions describing how to reach the treasure from a designated starting point (e.g., 1. First, start at the front door, 2. Second, take nine big steps forward, 3. Third, turn left at the bookshelf). These models will help introduce children to how maps and directions work, setting clear expectations for the activity.

Whole group discussion. Show the children different kinds of maps, including examples from books or online and the one you created of the early learning setting. Begin a discussion about the concept and purpose of maps, asking questions to evaluate children's experience and encourage them to share their understanding (e.g., "What do you think a map is for?," "Have you ever used a map before?"). Using the teacher-created classroom map, show how features marked on the map translate to the real world, focusing on spatial relationships between locations and representation of distance. Illustrate using the map to find the treasure. When children are familiar with this task, introduce the use of step-by-step directions alongside the map to give them an even more specific way to navigate the route to the treasure.

How to Play

This learning experience involves multiple steps and can be carried out over several days, depending on the children's level of interest and understanding. After the initial whole group discussion, split the group into two teams: mapmakers and treasure hunters. The first group creates and organizes maps, while the second becomes map interpreters and navigates the maps and directions to find the treasure. The teacher should ensure that all children have the opportunity to experience both roles.

Working individually or in small groups, mapmakers hide treasure and then create detailed maps of the early learning setting. As needed, the teacher can facilitate this work, such as prompting children to include familiar furniture and features (e.g., the teacher's desk, the whole group rug area) to accurately represent the layout of the learning setting and better help the treasure hunters in identifying the directions and locations of different learning centers. When discussing what should be included on the map and why they are important, depending on the children's capability, either the teacher or the children can draw additional furniture and features. Alternately, precut pictures or laminated picture cards with Velcro can be attached in place by the children. Once the map is complete, the treasure's location can be marked on the map with a sticker (e.g., a star, a treasure chest). Next, mapmakers create directions by describing the route to the treasure in three to five simple steps using words, symbols, and pictures. Preschool children have a limited capacity to store multiple steps in their working memory, so keeping steps short helps them succeed without feeling overwhelmed (Gathercole & Alloway 2008). Encourage children to use ordinal words (e.g., *first, second, third*) and directional words (e.g., *left, right, forward*) to structure the information clearly. This process helps children break down the task into manageable steps while ensuring the treasure hunters can follow the route effectively. By combining visual elements with clear language, children practice organizing and presenting information in a logical and accessible way.

With maps and directions in hand, treasure hunters navigate to locate the treasure. As a first step, encourage children to review the map to identify locations and landmarks. Then invite them to review the sequence of steps to make sure they understand them all and pay attention to the order. With this information, treasure hunters can plan out their route. One way to do this might be by using their finger to trace the path along the map according to the directions. When treasure hunters are ready, they can move to navigate the space with their bodies and see if they are able to locate the treasure. Teachers can facilitate collaboration by ensuring mapmakers communicate their instructions clearly and treasure hunters provide feedback as they interpret the map.

CT skill(s) and concept(s) engaged: decomposition / sequencing and logical order; abstraction / identifying important features and representation; algorithmic thinking / following directions and debugging

See It in Action

Making and Following a Map with Ms. Asami

Ms. Asami: Today, we are going to create a treasure map. Here's a map I made of our classroom. Who has heard of a map before? (*Waits and listens to a few of the children's positive responses*.) What is a map? What does it tell us?

Kim: A map is pictures. My dad has a map on his phone.

Ms. Asami: That's right, Kim! A map is a type of picture that shows us where things are. A map can be on a screen, like a phone, or on paper, like this one. (*Shows the model map of the early learning setting*.) If someone new joins our class or comes to visit, this map could help them find places in our classroom, like the literacy learning center or the dramatic play center. (*Holds additional discussion with the children about maps*.) Let's create a classroom map together. We'll start by placing some pictures of our classroom furniture on this big piece of paper. Here's a picture of my desk. Where should we put it on our map?

John: By the door!

Ms. Asami: Why don't you come and show me exactly where? We'll see if everyone agrees, and then you can glue it to our map.

Hank: I know where the science center goes—it's right next to your desk.

Ms. Asami: It is! Why don't we place that on our map next? Come on up. (*Continues to lead the discussion with the children on locations of various furniture and features until the map is completed.*) Now, let's play a game. One of you will hide a treasure—(*Holds up a teddy bear.*)—somewhere in the classroom. After, that person will mark the hiding spot on the map with a sticker. Then, the rest of us will use the map to find the treasure. Bindi, I saw you raise your hand. Would you like to be our treasure hider?

Bindi: Yes, I know the perfect spot! (*Takes the teddy bear and carefully hides it while the other children close their eyes. Places a sticker on the map to mark the treasure's location.*)

Ms. Asami: All right, everyone! Let's open our eyes and take a look at the map. Can anyone see where the treasure is hidden?

Esther: It looks like it's near the art center!

Ms. Asami: That's a great observation, Esther. Let's walk over together and check it out. Remember, use the map to guide you. What landmark do we need to look for first?

Ravi: The table—it's before the art center on the map! (*Points to the table as the other children gather around the map, some tracing their fingers along the route to the treasure.*)

Ms. Asami: Let's follow Ravi's lead. Everyone, keep looking at the map as we walk. What do we pass after the table?

Hank: The bookshelf! It's right here on the map.

Ms. Asami: Wonderful job! Are we getting close to the treasure?

John: It's near the corner by the easel—I see it on the map!

All children: (*Excitedly walk to the corner and find the teddy bear hidden behind the easel.*) We found it!

Ms. Asami: Excellent work! You used the map to find the treasure step by step.

Conclusion

By embedding CT skills and concepts into everyday experiences, educators create a rich environment that supports not only computational thinking but also broader aspects of children's development. This approach helps children build a strong foundation in problem solving, nurturing their ability to think creatively and efficiently. The intentional integration of CT into daily routines and learning centers and the introduction of targeted learning experiences prepare children to use these skills and concepts in a variety of contexts. By blending familiar routines and meaningful learning experiences with targeted experiences, children gain a well-rounded foundation in computational thinking.

CHAPTER 4

Coding Using Stories as a Framework

Thought Questions

- How is coding related to computational thinking?
- Why is it important to teach young children early coding?
- Why do stories serve as an effective framework for coding in early childhood?

Coding—the process of assigning instructions, or a code, to a machine or human to perform specific actions and complete tasks—is widely recognized as one of the most effective ways for children to practice their computational thinking skills (Lee 2020; McLennan 2017). In many ways, coding and computational thinking are closely intertwined. As discussed extensively in previous chapters, key aspects of CT include decomposition, or breaking down complex problems into manageable parts; abstraction, or ignoring unnecessary information while focusing on what is essential; pattern recognition, or identifying similarities and recurring elements; and algorithmic thinking, or developing step-by-step solutions (Lee 2020; Wing 2006). All of these skills are directly applied in the coding process. When coding (also known as programming), typically a specific programming language is used to write instructions in a way that computers can understand and carry out. This language serves as an algorithm for the computer, detailing step by step exactly what actions it needs to take. Once written, a computer can quickly scan and execute the algorithm, performing the required tasks with speed and precision (Resnick et al. 2009). The goal of coding is to develop the most effective and efficient algorithm to solve a problem.

Considering all that this book has discussed so far about computational thinking, it is clear to see how engaging in coding serves as a practical application of CT. Beyond CT, the coding process fosters a wide range of skills that are transferable across various scenarios in the learning environment and the real world. For example, when coding, children practice mathematical skills (e.g., counting, spatial sense) as well as scientific inquiry skills (e.g., observation, planning and conducting, communication, predicting) (Lee 2020). They are also encouraged to implement and iterate algorithms or solutions based on test results. By engaging in learning experiences that involve coding, children learn how to develop an algorithm to solve a problem or complete a task. Moreover, if their algorithm does not work, they can practice figuring out why and how it went wrong and coming up with ideas to fix those errors. This, in turn, promotes resilience and creativity. Together, these skills serve as a valuable set of tools for practicing a mindset that is analytical, systematic, and adaptable to new challenges (Brennan & Resnick 2012). In short, teaching young children the basic principles of coding helps them become better problem solvers.

This chapter explores what coding looks like and how it's talked about in early childhood specifically when using stories as a medium. It also overviews developmentally appropriate strategies for extending coding learning experiences.

Making Coding Meaningful in Early Childhood

Introducing coding concepts in ways that young learners can enjoy and understand is essential. It allows children to apply CT skills while teachers ensure that the experiences remain playful, engaging, and aligned with their learning needs (NAEYC 2020). One of the most effective methods for integrating coding is stories. Stories, whether found in children's books or drawn from children's imaginations and personal life experiences, are already a cornerstone of the early childhood curriculum, and with good reason. Their proven potential to help children learn new ideas and information is enormous (Bishop 1990; Labadie, Pole, & Rogers 2013; Wanless & Crawford 2016). By tapping into a medium that is already familiar to and beloved by children (stories) and connecting it to new knowledge (coding), educators can create and provide contextualized learning opportunities that are responsive to children's development, interests, and cultures (Joswick et al. 2023; Lee 2020).

Young children engage with stories in a variety of ways, and these interactions directly impact how stories can be used as a framework for coding. Teachers often read aloud to small or whole groups. This guided experience helps children see the events of a story unfold in sequence, building their understanding of a narrative structure with a beginning, middle, and end. Through repeated readings and scaffolded discussions, children begin to recognize patterns (e.g., cause-and-effect relationships), identify key events, and break down complex ideas from stories. Children may also choose to read independently during self-guided play or other times. When children interact with books on their own, their approach often differs from the conventional reading methods used by adults. Instead of reading all text from cover to cover, children may focus on illustrations, make guesses about the story, or even create their own narratives based on the images they see. This exploratory process allows children to focus on information they identify as important, analyze events at their own pace, and piece together original stories based on logical connections. These early reading behaviors are vital for developing children's literacy skills and are encouraged because they lay the foundation for becoming proficient readers. They also naturally align with the four major skills of computational thinking. In this way, story engagement acts as a developmental bridge to CT, making stories an ideal entry point for introducing coding concepts.

> Coding with stories can be practiced through both unplugged and plugged learning experiences, but maintaining a balance is essential. In considering children's cognitive development, their interests, and how they learn best at this age, it is most effective to begin with unplugged learning experiences.

To code a story, children identify and sequence major narrative events. This process mirrors children's natural tendencies to break down and reconstruct narratives. Coding with stories can be practiced through both unplugged and plugged learning experiences, but maintaining a balance is essential. In considering children's cognitive development, their interests, and how they learn best at this age, it is most effective to begin with unplugged learning experiences. As discussed in previous chapters, preschoolers are still developing abstract thinking skills (Piaget 1952). The technology used in plugged learning experiences often involves abstract concepts and symbolic representations, such as directional arrows or numerical input. By first introducing children to these concepts and representations through unplugged learning experiences, children use concrete materials and hands-on engagement to actively see and touch their way to understanding their abstract foundations. This progression from concrete to abstract not only supports their cognitive development but also fosters a solid understanding of coding concepts.

How to Code Using Stories

The basic process of coding using stories typically follows these steps:

1. Create or select a story.
2. Create a picture card for each major narrative event.
3. Arrange the picture cards to establish the narrative's sequence.
4. Create a coding grid.
5. Place the picture cards on the coding grid in a random order.
6. Navigate a pathway on the coding grid.

Each step builds upon the last to help children develop CT skills while engaging with storytelling. Teachers should plan and prepare for these steps in advance while leaving room for collaborative exploration with children.

These steps are explored in more detail in the sections that follow, including how each can be adapted to various levels of complexity to meet children where they are developmentally.

Step One: Select or Create a Story

Stories as a basis for coding learning experiences can be drawn from different sources. This chapter focuses on two: stories from children's books and stories based on children's interests or personal experiences. These categories represent two distinct approaches, each with their own unique considerations.

It is recommended to begin with the first category, selecting stories from children's books. This approach is typically a more accessible starting point for teachers and children as it provides a clear framework for introducing coding concepts without the added challenge of creating a story from scratch. When selecting a book, educators should carefully plan and review to ensure the story is high quality, aligns with the learning objectives, and meets the diverse needs of the group. Collins and Schickedanz (2024) outline six key criteria to consider: complexity, potential interest to young children, richness of language, values conveyed, representation of diversity and inclusivity, and appropriateness of illustrations. For the purpose of coding a story, this book expands upon and adapts some of these criteria as follows:

- Prioritize books with a clear narrative structure, such as a well-defined beginning, middle, and end. These lend themselves more effectively to coding tasks like sequencing and algorithmic thinking.
- Select stories with themes, language, and complexity appropriate for the developmental level of the children.
- Choose books that expose children to rich, expressive language, fostering both literacy development and critical thinking.
- Look for stories that invite children to interact and engage by predicting outcomes, connecting events to personal experiences, or participating in discussions.
- Ensure stories reflect the cultural backgrounds and lived experiences of the children, promoting inclusivity and relatability.
- Seek out books with visuals that complement the text and help children understand and interpret the story's events.

By keeping these criteria in mind, the stories selected will not only support the development of CT and coding concepts but also contribute to children's learning and development in a range of other ways, from literacy development to understanding emotions.

Stories can range from a simple progression of events to a more complex narrative with a plot and characters. Younger preschoolers might start out with simple, linear stories that provide a clear structure that is easier to deconstruct, sequence, and translate into coding. As children become more familiar with coding stories, educators can gradually introduce more complex narratives. Stories with multiple characters, branching plotlines, or cause-and-effect relationships challenge children to think critically about the relationships between events and create more sophisticated coding pathways.

Accurate representation of diversity and inclusivity in both contents and illustrations is an especially important consideration. Books, like any other materials incorporated in the early learning environment, offer opportunities to expose children to diverse cultures, languages, family structures, abilities, and more. This promotes a sense of community and belonging as well as the acceptance and celebration of differences, which in turn makes learning more relevant and meaningful (Wanless & Crawford 2016).

Once children become comfortable coding preexisting stories, educators can fold in story creation, the second approach, as a way to extend children's learning and encourage deeper engagement. Story creation involves children actively crafting their own stories, which fosters creativity and allows them to take ownership of the process. Stories based on children's interests and experiences naturally engage children because they get to see things they do in their daily life or take joy in reflected back at them. This could include cleaning up play materials at the end of the day, going outside on a nature walk, following a day in the life of a dinosaur, and more.

Teachers might co-create these stories with the child or the child might create one entirely on their own, depending on the child's developmental skills, prior experience with storytelling, and comfort level with the activity. Co-creating stories is a highly effective starting point, especially for younger children or those new to narrative construction. This collaborative process allows educators to model key storytelling techniques, such as sequencing and character development. Co-creation also fosters a sense of partnership, encouraging the child to actively contribute while still feeling supported. As children become more proficient, transition to independent story creation, which provides an opportunity for children to exercise greater autonomy, creativity, and problem-solving skills. The shift from co-creation to independent creation can be tailored to each child's readiness, ensuring the activity remains developmentally appropriate and engaging.

Step Two: Create a Picture Card for Each Major Narrative Event

After sharing a story, it is important to engage children in discussing its major events. As educators prompt children to recall and retell what happened in the story, introduce the idea of creating picture cards to represent each event. Picture cards serve as visual cues to help children retell the story. They are a versatile tool for breaking down the larger plot into smaller parts (decomposition), recognizing which events are critical to the narrative (abstraction), and beginning to establish the sequence of events (algorithmic thinking). The last of these is discussed further in step three.

Each picture card should feature a simple, recognizable drawing or photograph that clearly represents a single major story event. (See Figure 4.1.) Images are the primary means of representation for preschoolers because they are still emergent readers. That said, if some children are familiar with certain words, those words might also be integrated into the picture cards (e.g., a picture of a fox and the word *fox* written just beneath it). This approach supports both visual learning and early literacy development.

Depending on the developmental level of the children, picture cards can be prepared in advance by teachers, created by the children, or some combination of the two. Various materials can be used to create picture cards, but some staples include blank index cards (or some other thick, durable paper) and markers, crayons, or colored pencils. As needed, you might support children in creating picture cards by providing preprinted images for them to cut out and glue on index cards. Consider laminating the completed picture cards for reuse across multiple coding learning experiences.

As a starting point, two to four major story events should be highlighted, meaning there will be two to four corresponding picture cards. As children become more comfortable with the learning experience and their ability to manage greater complexity grows, this range can gradually increase to five to 10 events and cards.

Figure 4.1 Picture Cards Representing Major Story Events

These picture cards might be used to represent major events in a story like the following: *Lainy the mouse ate an orange in the morning for breakfast, a bunch of grapes at noon for lunch, and a watermelon in the evening for dinner.*

Step Three: Arrange the Picture Cards to Establish the Narrative's Sequence

With the major events of a story identified and picture cards created, teachers pivot their conversations and interactions with children to guide them in sequencing those events. While the approach and questions used to scaffold this task may differ slightly between stories from books versus stories created by children, the primary purpose remains the same: to establish the narrative's sequence and order the picture cards to reflect that sequence.

In the case of stories from children's books, teachers focus more on helping children to recall and organize an existing sequence. When children determined a story's major events in the previous step, those events might have been brought up in order or out of order. Now, with the picture cards on hand, the narrative's sequence of events is reviewed again and established or reinforced by placing the picture cards on an anchor chart. Questions like "What did the character do first?" and "What happened next?" guide children to analyze the story structure. The overall discussion draws more heavily on comprehension and memory skills.

Consider the book *There's a Bear on My Chair*, by Ross Collins. The story features a mouse who becomes increasingly frustrated because a big bear is sitting in his chair. Its sequence of events unfolds as follows: the mouse sees a bear on his chair, he tries different ways to get the bear to move, he becomes increasingly dramatic in his efforts, and he eventually gives up and leaves—only to end up sitting in the bear's bed. After sharing the story, a teacher can discuss these key events with the children and lead a discussion in which they arrange the events in the correct order together, establishing the narrative's sequence and creating an anchor chart. This method helps children understand the story's chain of events, a key part of coding the story. The completed anchor chart serves as a concrete material that children can reference later as they get further along in their coding work.

On the other hand, with stories created by children, conversations are child driven and more exploratory. Teachers ask questions like "What happens next in your story?" and "How does the story end?" to prompt children to give their narrative structure. These discussions may involve negotiating the narrative as children decide on their own story's events and sequence, which can initially be fluid. Through guidance, teachers can help children solidify their intended order of events. For instance, for a child-created story about a mouse named Lainy who eats a series of fruits, the teacher might guide the child to identify and arrange the sequence of fruits eaten—an orange for breakfast, grapes for lunch, and a watermelon for dinner—by referencing the picture cards and discussing their order. Here again, an anchor chart is a useful tool to establish a final sequence that can be consulted later.

For all stories, these discussions not only enhance sequencing skills but also connect to broader concepts like coding, emphasizing the importance of arranging events accurately in a logical order.

Step Four: Create a Coding Grid

A coding grid or matrix is a tool to visually organize the sequence of story events in a structured way. (This is discussed further in step five.) Coding grids with various dimensions—that is, number of rows and columns—can be created based on the children's cognitive levels and familiarity with this learning experience. When children first begin, it is recommended to start with smaller dimensions, such as a one-dimensional coding grid with one row and enough cells to accommodate the number of story events. A three-by-three grid works well as the baseline dimension for preschoolers who have some exposure to this learning experience. As children become more experienced and are ready to explore more complex pathways in a bigger space, larger grid layouts can be introduced (e.g., four by four, five by five). The more dimensions a coding grid has, the more challenging it will be. However, additional dimensions also provide children with greater flexibility to design algorithms and encourage them to create the most efficient solutions using the fewest steps. For preschoolers, the grid layout can extend to eight by eight (or sometimes further), but this should only be introduced if children fully grasp this learning experience and need more of a challenge.

Teachers can create coding grids in advance or involve children in the process. Engaging children provides a hands-on learning opportunity, reinforcing their understanding of organization and sequencing. That said, children may not be ready to participate meaningfully in this task until they have some familiarity with coding stories. There are a variety of options when creating grids, and the choice of materials and approach can greatly influence the learning experience. For a more traditional strategy, standard-size paper (laminated for reuse) and markers can be used, especially if children are working individually or in small groups. When working with a whole group, the whiteboard is a space that is easily viewable by and accessible to most children. For a more physically interactive experience, you might adapt the size of the grid to be big enough for children to navigate with their own bodies rather than their fingers or writing tools. To create a large-scale coding grid, sketch it with a marker on butcher paper, outline it in tape on carpet, or draw it with chalk on outdoor pavement.

Step Five: Place the Picture Cards on the Coding Grid in a Random Order

Place the picture cards representing the major events of a story on the coding grid in a random order (see Figure 4.2). Educators can choose to complete this step independently or involve children in the process. In the case of the latter, educators can provide prompts (e.g., "Where should we place the orange?") or step-by-step guidance as needed.

Figure 4.2 Three-by-Three Coding Grid with Picture Cards Arranged in a Random Order

Rearranging the picture cards periodically on the same grid dimensions challenges children to develop new algorithms and explore multiple solutions. This flexibility reinforces their adaptability and problem-solving skills. See step six for further exploration of this point. As children become more experienced, educators can create more complex picture card arrangements. More advanced grids may also include irrelevant picture cards as obstacles to increase the challenge. This requires children to engage in abstraction, ignoring unnecessary information (irrelevant picture cards) and concentrating only on the actual events that happened in the story. For example, if a banana picture card is added as an obstacle (see Figure 4.3), children must learn to navigate around it while

Figure 4.3 Coding Grid with Picture Cards, Including an Obstacle (Irrelevant Picture Card)

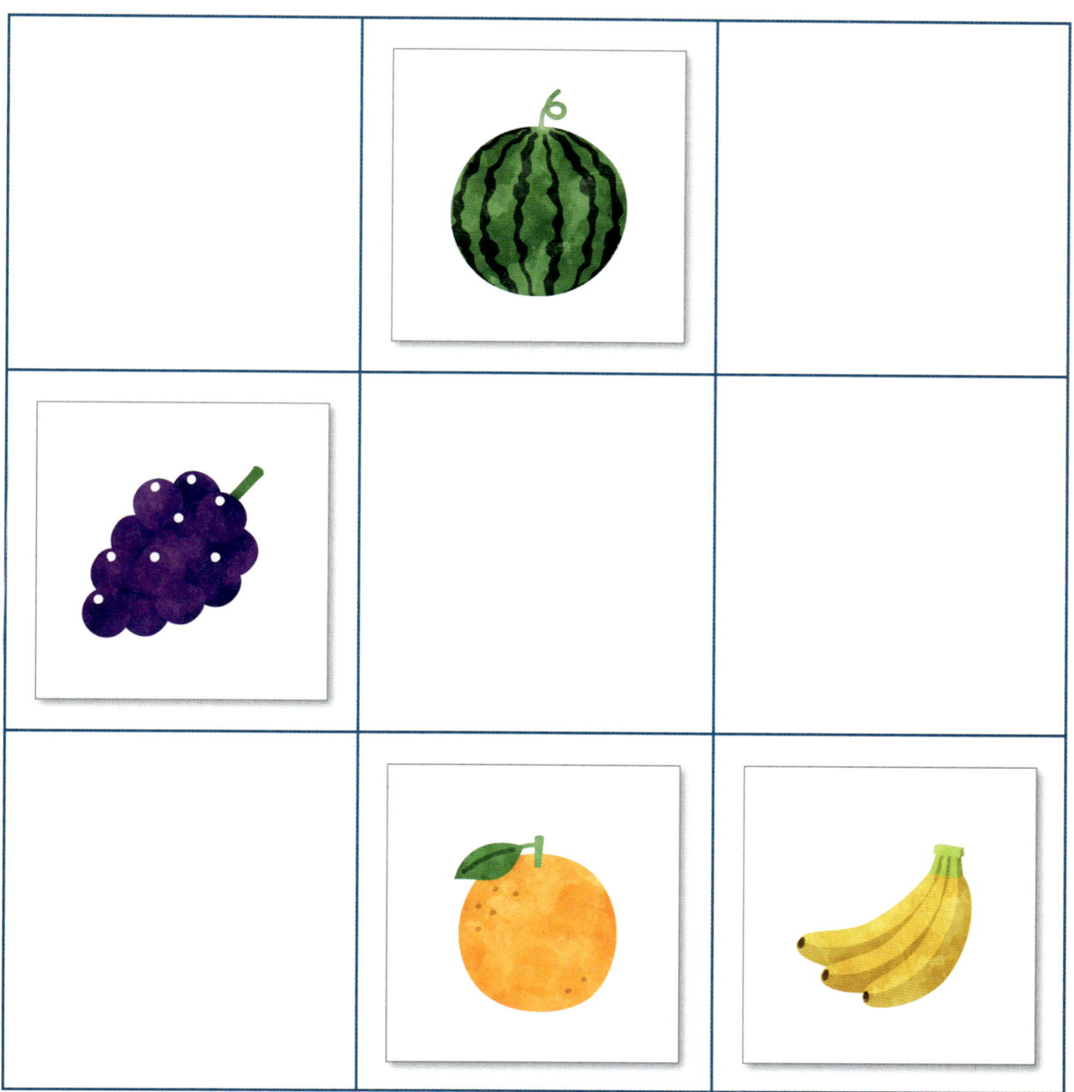

focusing only on a pathway (algorithm) that touches on the relevant events (the orange, the grapes, and the watermelon).

Educators should ensure that the challenges remain developmentally appropriate and avoid overwhelming children with excessive obstacles or overly complex layouts too soon. A gradual progression from simpler tasks to more advanced ones supports children's confidence and skill development while making story coding an enjoyable learning experience.

Step Six: Navigate a Pathway on the Coding Grid

With the picture cards scattered on the coding grid, it is time for children to forge a path, or create an algorithm, that touches on each story event in the correct sequence. The anchor chart created in step three is a helpful resource for children to reference at this stage. At first, children may find it easiest to create a pathway by identifying a distinct starting location for the story's main character. A figurine, picture card, or some other material representing the story's main character can be placed on an empty square of the grid. Children can then plot out the character's pathway by drawing a continuous line or moving the character through each event in sequence (see Figure 4.4). Both approaches allow children to visually and physically navigate through the narrative's progression, which helps them see how each event is connected to the next. It also supports them in recognizing that while there may be variations, they generally must follow a specific path to successfully move from a story's beginning to its end in the correct order.

Once a child feels comfortable drawing lines or moving figurines for their pathways, they can advance to using arrow cards or stickers. In the context of coding stories, arrow cards represent the direction and flow of events in a story (see Figure 4.5). Before marking anything on the coding grid, children need to pause and think carefully about the order of events and how each event leads into the next. Drawing a line or moving a figurine often feels more intuitive to children and therefore might not require the same level of thoughtful planning. Arrow cards encourage them to slow down, reflect, and make deliberate choices, just as someone would when writing simple code to execute a task. By using arrows to indicate movement toward story events, children are also introduced to symbolic representation, which is a key part of both reading and coding. In other words, children must mentally visualize and understand the movement represented by an arrow card, rather than relying on physically moving their hand to guide a marker or figurine along the intended path.

Just as the arrow cards symbolize movement in the story, in coding, symbols are used to represent actions, directions, and commands. Incorporating arrow cards integrates basic coding principles, such as directionality and sequencing, in a hands-on and engaging way. This connection between the physical action of placing arrows and the abstract idea of directing movement is foundational for developing computational thinking. Additionally, placing arrows on a grid and rotating them to indicate the intended direction involves a spatial thinking component, helping children develop an awareness of where an object is located in relation to another object (Lee 2016). Spatial awareness allows children to mentally visualize how objects fit together, move, or interact in a given space. As they develop this skill, they learn to predict outcomes, like how a left turn differs from a right turn or how forward movement changes depending on orientation. Spatial thinking is essential not only for coding but also for understanding relationships between objects, navigating space, and solving problems in everyday life.

Figure 4.4 Coding Grid with Picture Cards for Major Events and the Main Character with a Pathway Indicated by a Drawn Line

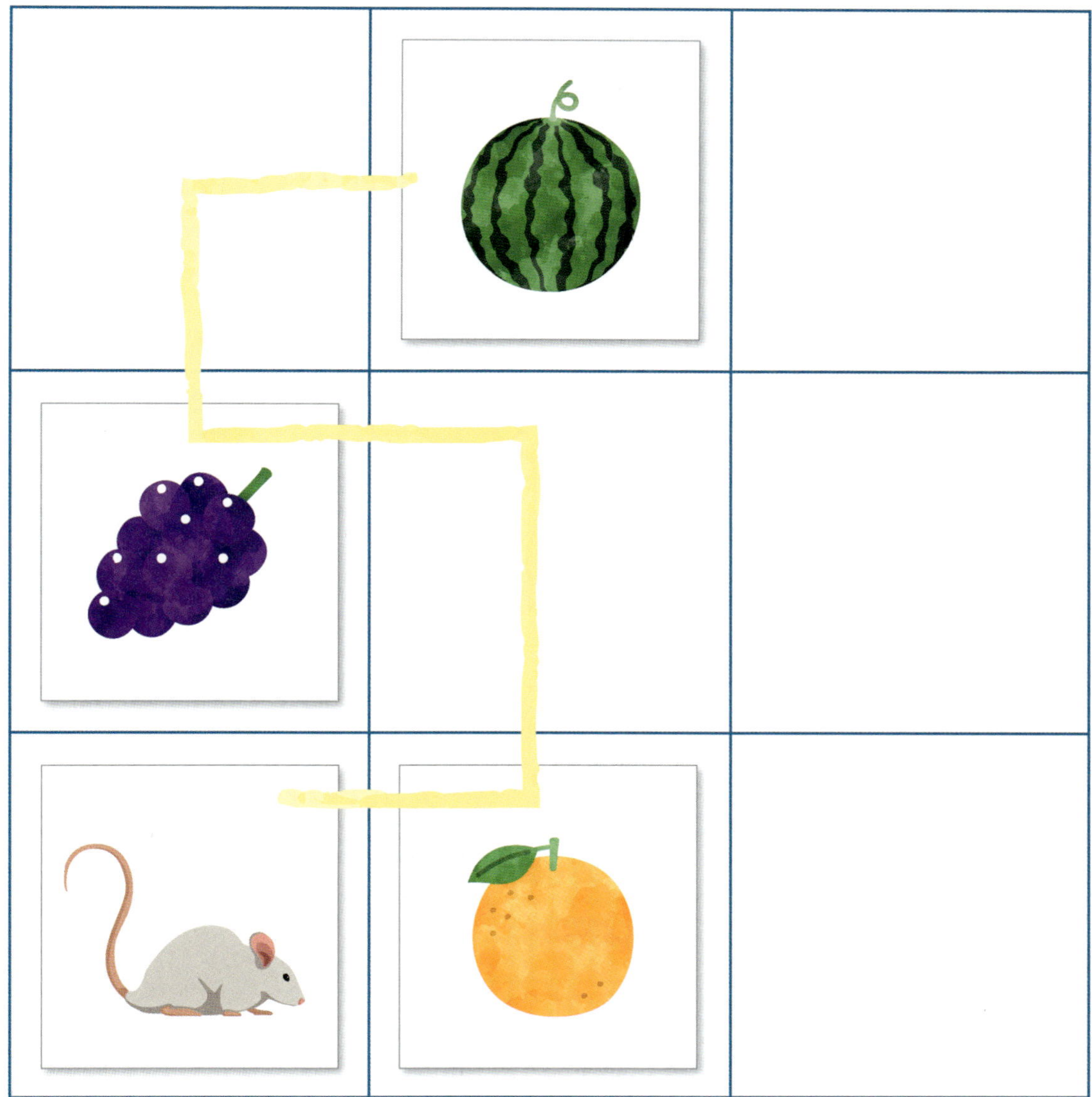

Occasionally, children may come up with different algorithms when presented with the same exact coding grid dimensions and picture card arrangement. Figures 4.6 and 4.7 show two examples of this. The more dimensions a coding grid has, the more potential algorithm variations there can be. That said, some algorithms are more streamlined or efficient than others. When children find multiple pathways, it provides valuable opportunities to share, explore, and compare algorithms.

Figure 4.5 Coding Grid with Picture Cards and a Pathway Indicated by Arrow Cards

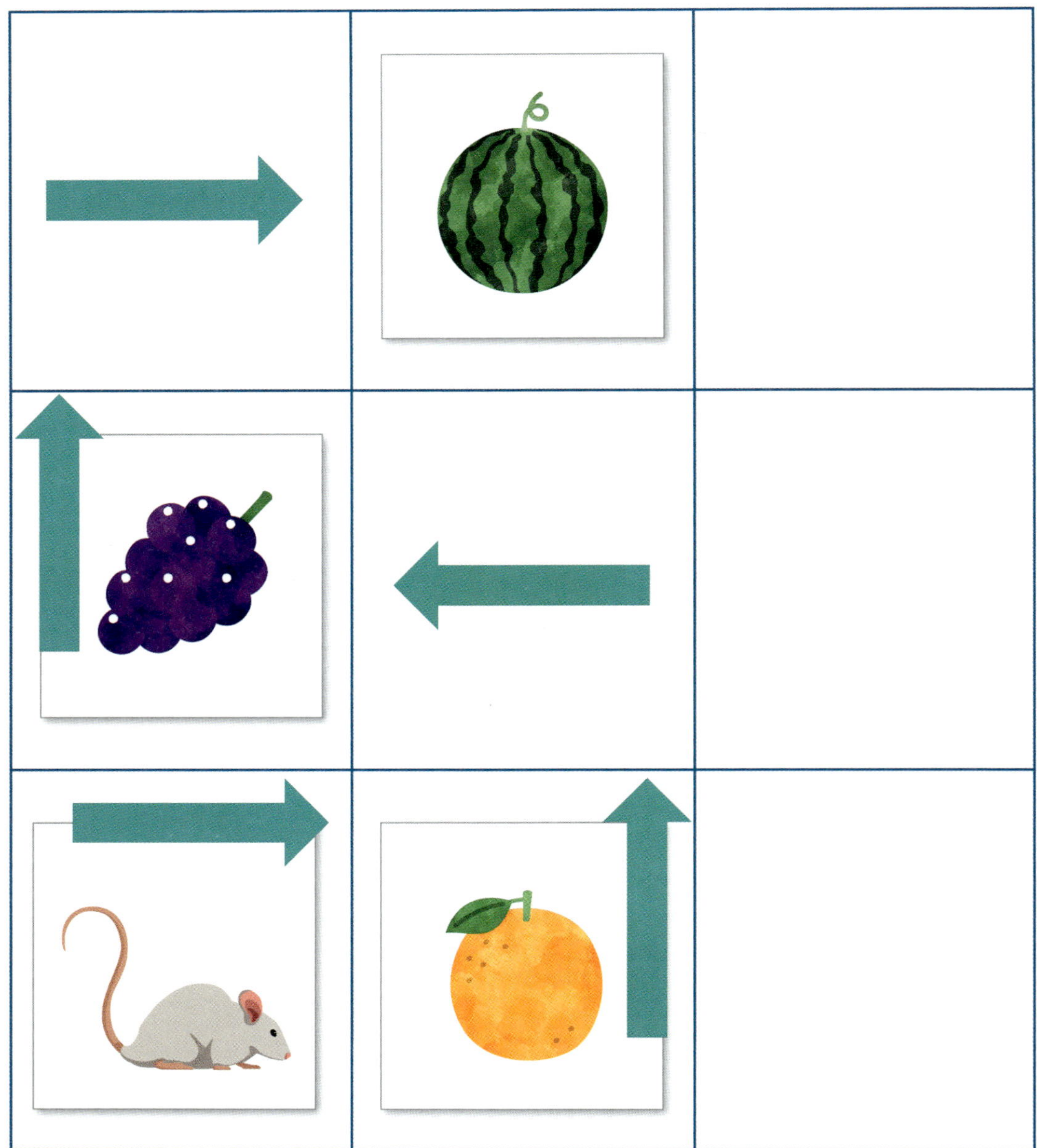

As part of these comparisons, teachers might encourage children to count the number of steps—whether represented by grid cells when drawing lines or by arrow cards—that each of their algorithms needed to achieve the desired outcome. They can then compare and identify which required the fewest steps. Discussions around these explorations prompt children to think more

Figure 4.6 Two Different Algorithms on a Three-by-Three Coding Grid

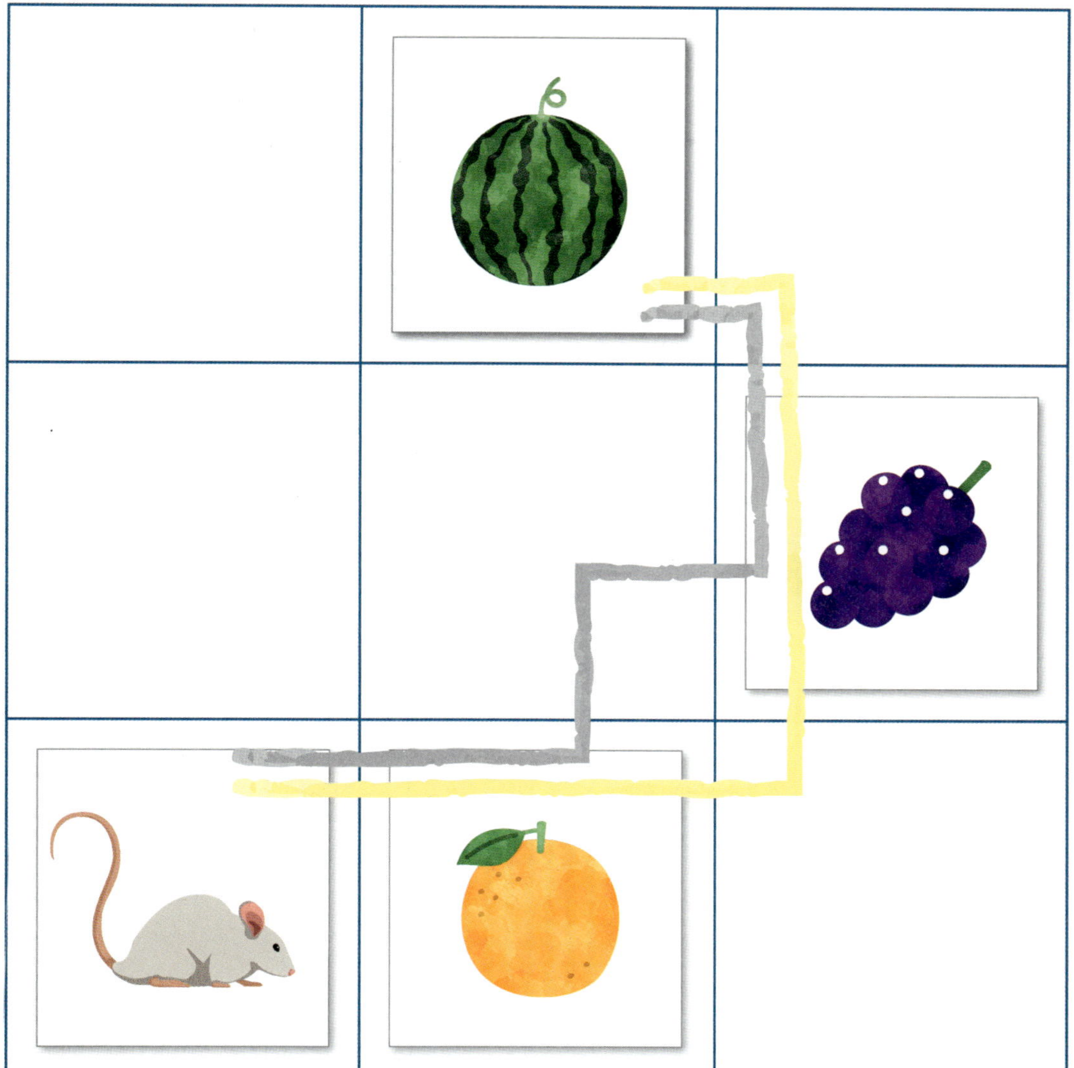

The drawn lines in gray and yellow show two different pathways that children created. While they differ slightly, both are correct because all major story events are touched in the established sequence.

deeply about their own algorithm, to articulate that thinking to justify their choices, and to consider alternatives they might not have previously seen. When scaffolded intentionally by an educator, conversations like these shape more sophisticated critical reasoning skills as well as more strategic and creative problem-solving approaches. In turn, children form the understanding that an algorithm should not only achieve the expected outcome but also be as efficient as possible.

Figure 4.7 Four Different Algorithms on a Four-by-Four Coding Grid

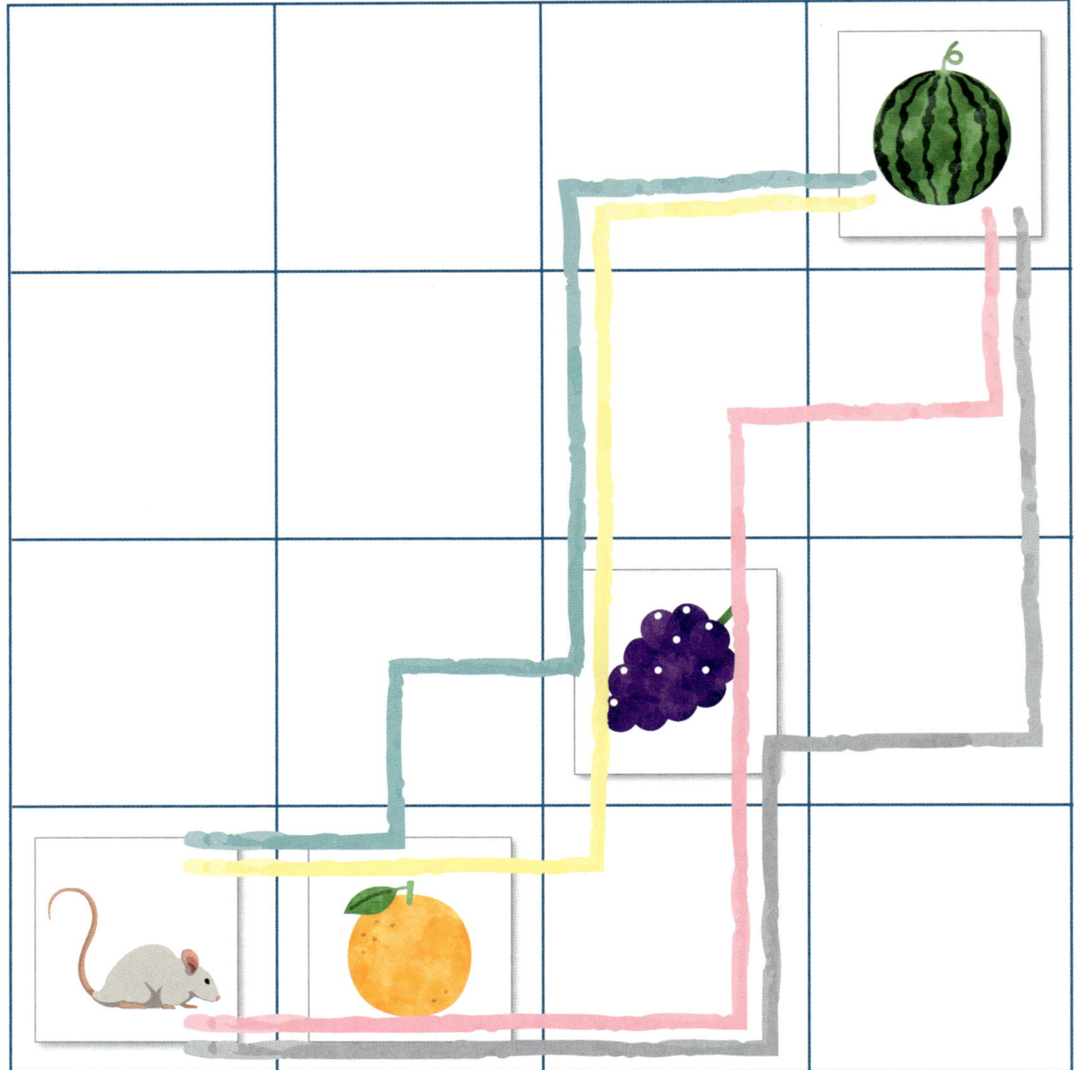

The drawn lines in blue, yellow, gray, and pink show four different pathways that children created.

CT Terms and Other Language Commonly Used When Coding Using Stories

When children code using stories, integrating relevant terms helps them organize the given information and connects the storytelling process to fundamental coding concepts, creating a bridge between storytelling and computational thinking. To make these terms meaningful for children, it is key to model their use in discussions and actively encourage children to do the same. The following sections overview some terms that are commonly used when coding and feature vignettes to showcase contextualized scenarios for how those words can be embedded in your conversations with young children.

Sequential Words

Sequential words, also known as transitional words, are used to describe the order of events and when they happen in relation to one another. This category of terms includes ordinal words (e.g., *first, second, third*) and time-order words (e.g., *next, after, before*). When explaining sequences, using sequential words in your discussions with children helps them understand the order of major events in a story and reinforces how language can be used to clearly communicate their logical progression.

Ms. Erica Facilitates a Discussion About the Sequence of Major Events in a Story

Ms. Erica shares a story with the children about a group of friends spending the day at the beach, during which they swim, have a picnic, and build sandcastles. After finishing the story, Ms. Erica and the children identify the major events and make picture cards for each one. Now, she leads them in a conversation about the story's sequence so they can create an anchor chart together.

Ms. Erica: Hmm, I can't remember. What did the friends do first at the beach?

Linus: Swim.

Ms. Erica: Oh yes, that's it! They swam first. (*Shows the picture card of the sea and places it on the anchor chart affixed to the board.*) What did they do second?

Zhu Li: A picnic.

Ms. Erica: That sounds right—they had a picnic lunch. (*Places the picture card of the picnic basket on the anchor chart.*) What did they do last?

Arthur: (*Loudly.*) Sandcastles!

Ms. Erica: Well done. (*Places the picture card of the sandcastle on the anchor chart.*) And that's our last part of the story. Let's go over what happened one more time. (*Points to each picture card on the anchor chart while retelling the story.*) First, the friends went swimming in the sea. Then, they had a picnic for their lunch. And finally, they built sandcastles.

Directional Words

Directional words describe the location of something relative to other objects. These terms indicate spatial relationships and are particularly significant in coding stories. While the category encompasses a broader array of terms that indicate direction in space, for the purposes of story coding, the most relevant are *left, right, up,* and *down*. When first beginning to talk about where

Figure 4.8 Ways to Bring the Infant a Rattle

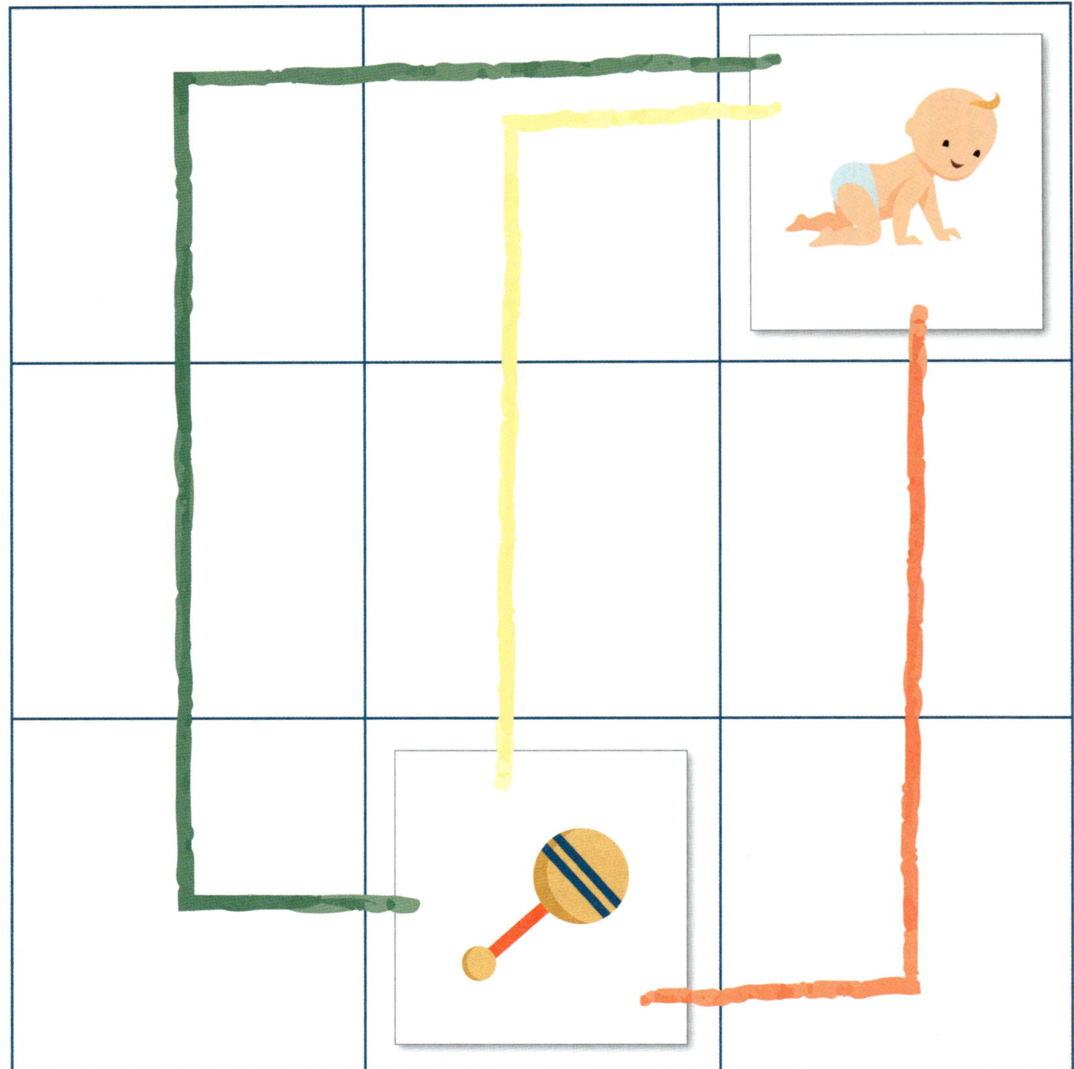

Samantha's algorithm is indicated by the red line, Noam's by the yellow line, and Katia's by the green line.

something is, children often rely on vague language like *here* and *there*. Story coding provides valuable opportunities to introduce them to more specific directional terminology and how accurately organizing and presenting information using that terminology is crucial to successful navigation of a space, whether that's a coding grid or the environment around them. Repeated exposure to specific directional words helps children to become familiar with and associate those words with the corresponding directions. In turn, they will gradually start using them appropriately over time.

When using directional words with young children, it is strongly recommended that the teacher face the same way as the children do. This allows both the teacher and the children to have a consistent point of reference when indicating directions. Facing the opposite way of the children can cause confusion unless the teacher is careful to use directional words from the children's perspective.

Mr. Mikhail Uses Directional Words to Help Children Describe Their Algorithms

Samantha and Noam are looking at the coding grid their teacher, Mr. Mikhail, has given them (see Figure 4.8). After a whole group discussion in which a story about an infant who wants a rattle was shared and discussed, the children were put in pairs to resolve the problem together. While the children are mid-conversation about what to do, Mr. Mikhail stops to listen in.

Samantha: We go this way. (*Points her finger at the picture of the rattle and moves it to the right.*) One.

Mr. Mikhail: You mean to the right?

Samantha: Yes, to the right.

Noam: Yeah. (*Nods.*) Yes.

Samantha: Now, we go this way. (*Moves her finger up toward the picture of the infant, tapping each cell and counting aloud.*) One, two, three.

Mr. Mikhail: Great! So, you want to move the rattle up three steps?

Samantha: Yeah. The baby has the toy. (*Smiles proudly.*)

Noam: (*Laughs excitedly.*) The baby got the toy!

Mr. Mikhail: Great job! Can you show me again how you did it?

Samantha: Yes, I can! First, we go here. (*Points to the picture of the rattle.*) And then we go here. (*Points to the cell on the right.*)

Mr. Mikhail: So first you moved the rattle one step to the right? (*Traces his finger from the cell with the rattle to the empty cell to its right.*)

Samantha: Yes. (*Nods.*) And then we move up and give it to the baby. (*Begins counting.*) One, two, thr—oh, two times.

Mr. Mikhail: Oh, I see! You moved the rattle up *two* times to get it to the baby?

Samantha: Yes.

Mr. Mikhail: Wow, you did an amazing job bringing the toy to the baby! The baby should be very happy now. (*Looks at the coding grid.*) Hmm, I wonder if there's another way to bring the rattle to the baby. (*Pauses to allow the children space to think and explore.*)

Noam: I got it! I can bring the toy to the baby—it's different! See? From here, we go up this way. Two times. (*Points to the picture of the rattle and drags his finger to the cell at the top of the middle column.*) And then I can bring the toy to the baby. (*Moves his finger to the right.*)

Samantha: (*Smiles.*) Yeah.

Mr. Mikhail: Great thinking! You moved the rattle up two steps? (*Looks at Noam.*) Is that right?

Noam: Yes. Go this way. (*Points his finger to the right.*)

Mr. Mikhail: Then we go one step to the right?

Noam: One step to the right.

Mr. Mikhail: I like the way you found a different path! You're such a creative thinker.

Katia: (*Chimes in excitedly from the other side of the table.*) I have one!

Mr. Mikhail: You do? (*Circles to the other side of the table to look at Katia's coding grid with her.*) Can you share?

Katia: (*Uses her finger to start at the picture of the rattle.*) Uh huh. Go this way. (*Points to the cell on the left.*)

Mr. Mikhail: (*Rephrases.*) You move the rattle one step to the left?

Katia: Yes, to the left. And then go up two.

Mr. Mikhail: Great! (*Traces the pathway with his finger.*) You move the rattle up two steps?

Katia: Yes. (*Nods.*) And then go to the baby's side, two steps.

Mr. Mikhail: (*Smiles.*) Ah, you move the rattle two steps to the right, toward the baby? (*Traces the pathway with his finger.*)

Katia: Yes!

Mr. Mikhail: Wow, I'm very impressed! That is another creative way to bring the rattle to the baby.

Algorithm

This book has previously discussed and defined the word *algorithm* as a set of step-by-step instructions. While it might seem like a complex word for preschoolers, young children at this age are often excited to learn and use new or "big" words. When introducing this word while coding stories, it is helpful to use *algorithm* interchangeably with simpler terms like *pathways* or *ways*. For example, a teacher might say, "We are going to create a way, or an algorithm, for the turtle to reach the pond. An *algorithm* is a step-by-step procedure to help us figure out how to do that." This approach is also recommended when engaging in interactions with the children during discussions about their coding work. Instead of just asking "How did you do it?," you might ask your question in familiar language first and then immediately rephrase it using more complex terms, such as "Can you show me how you got there? What is your algorithm for how you did it?" This strategy makes the term meaningful, presents it in a playful and practical context, and fosters children's curiosity.

Mx. Jimenez Incorporates the Term *Algorithm* in a Discussion

After the children create their own algorithms based on the story of a turtle trying to reach a cool pond on a hot day, Mx. Jimenez calls them back to the rug for whole group discussion. They are asked to bring the coding grids showing their algorithms to the rug if they created one.

Mx. Jimenez: I'm so excited to talk about the algorithms you created based on the story about our turtle friend. Can anyone remind me what an algorithm is? (*Notices Faith raising her hand.*) Yes, Faith?

Faith: An algorithm is to find, umm . . . where the turtle go.

Mx. Jimenez: Great thinking, Faith! You explained what an algorithm is very well. For this story, the algorithm is the pathway the turtle followed. Does anyone else want to share what an algorithm might be?

Ilian: An algorithm is finding the ways the turtle goes through?

Mx. Jimenez: Exactly! An algorithm is about creating or finding the steps the turtle goes through to reach his end goal. You both did an excellent job explaining what an algorithm is. It's such a big word, and I'm glad you understand what it means. Now, who would like to share their own algorithm?

Ilian: (*Holds up his coding grid; see Figure 4.9.*)

Mx. Jimenez: Can you explain your algorithm to us?

Ilian: (*Points to a picture of the turtle on the grid.*) The turtle walked along the road. (*Traces his finger along the line through the picture card showing a road.*) Then he went into the woods. (*Traces his finger to the picture card with trees.*) And *then* he jumped into the pond! (*Reaches the picture card with the pond.*)

Mx. Jimenez: Wow, great job! The turtle moves three steps to the right and walks along the road. Next, he goes up one step, then takes two steps to the left, and up one more step to reach the woods. Finally, the turtle goes two steps up and one step right to jump into the pond. Is that right, Ilian? Is that your algorithm?

Ilian: Yes.

Mx. Jimenez: This is a great algorithm showing what the turtle did. Does anyone else have a different way or a different algorithm to share?

Figure 4.9 Illian's Algorithm for How the Turtle Reached the Pond

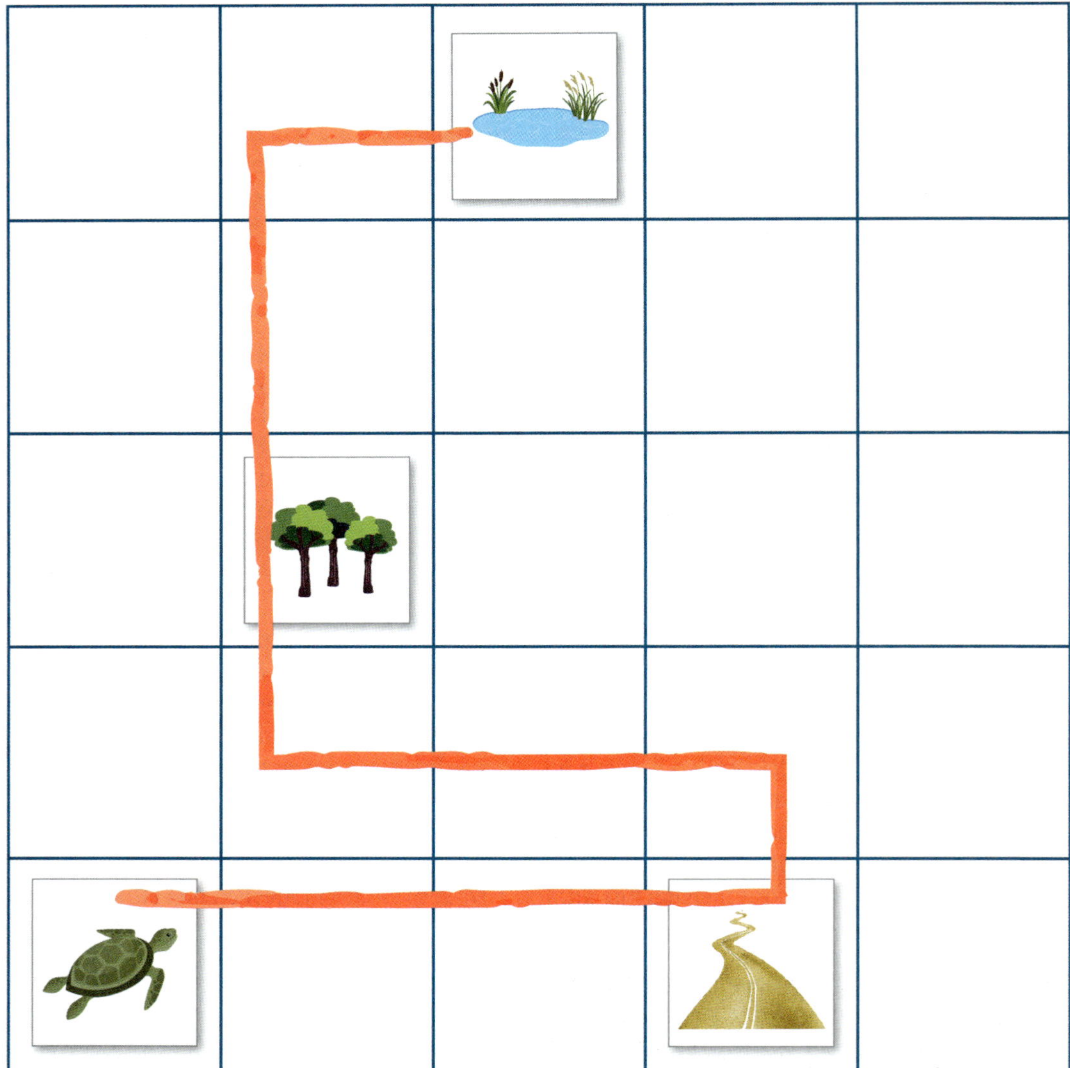

Debug

Debugging involves identifying and correcting errors—or bugs—to ensure that an algorithm functions as intended (Bers, González-González, & Armas–Torres 2019). When children code a story or create an algorithm, it's common for things not to work perfectly on the first try. Events might be reached out of sequence or missed entirely. Alternately, an obstacle like an irrelevant picture card might be incorporated into the algorithm and lead to an unexpected result. Encouraging children to be comfortable making mistakes and then learn how to fix them is an essential practice in coding as it teaches persistence, resilience, critical thinking, and problem solving.

Educators can guide children through the debugging process by asking them questions and making comments that prompt them to carefully observe their decisions, determine exactly what went wrong, and think about how to correct it. By encouraging children to analyze their steps, you help them specifically identify where their algorithm might have gone off course. This strategy can also be applied to children's daily activities, inviting them to identify and correct mistakes in tasks they engage in. By incorporating the term *debug* into everyday situations, children become familiar with it and begin to apply it naturally in their lives.

Teachers might also create opportunities for collaboration and a deeper understanding of debugging by having children share with each other how they fixed their mistakes. Hearing about errors made by others reinforces the idea that making mistakes is part of the problem-solving process. Consider the vignette on page 101 ("Mr. Mikhail Uses Directional Words to Help Children Describe Their Algorithms"). As Samantha navigated the path to get the rattle to the infant, she realized an error in her counting of cells and independently corrected it, demonstrating a form of debugging driven by her own reasoning but prompted by Mr. Mikhail's request for her to repeat her algorithm.

Mx. Jimenez Guides Hajun Through the Debugging Process

Another child in Mx. Jimenez's class, Hajun, is coding the same story about the turtle trying to reach the pond. On this day, the picture cards on the coding grid have been rearranged. There is also an irrelevant picture card included for an extra challenge. While creating his algorithm, Hajun accidentally draws a line through this obstacle, a picture of a hill, as shown in Figure 4.10 (left). Mx. Jimenez notices this and pauses to engage him in a one-on-one conversation.

Mx. Jimenez: Hajun, can you tell me about your algorithm? What did the turtle do?

Hajun: He walks by the road. (*Traces his finger from the picture card of the turtle to the one of the road.*) Then he . . . (*Traces his finger to the picture of the hill and pauses.*) Oh, no! He didn't go up a hill.

Mx. Jimenez: I think you're right. What should we do?

Hajun: Can I do it again? It's not right.

Mx. Jimenez: Of course! Do you want to fix your mistake? Do you want to debug your algorithm?

Hajun: Yes! (*Nods and wipes off his original drawn line. Draws an X over the picture of the hill.*) I smushed the bug! (*Laughs.*) The turtle didn't go up a hill. (*Draws a new line that follows the correct sequence of the story—road, woods, and pond—bypassing the hill picture card; see Figure 4.10 [right].*)

Mx. Jimenez: Great thinking! Did you remove the bug?

Hajun: Yep. I crossed out the hill.

Mx. Jimenez: Very good! I see it. Tell me about your new debugged algorithm.

Hajun: The turtle walks by the road. (*Traces his finger from the picture card of the turtle to the one of the road.*) Then he went to the woods. (*Traces his finger to the picture card with trees.*) And finally, he jumped in the pond. (*Moves his finger to the picture of the pond and taps on it.*)

Figure 4.10 Coding Grids Showing Debugging in Action

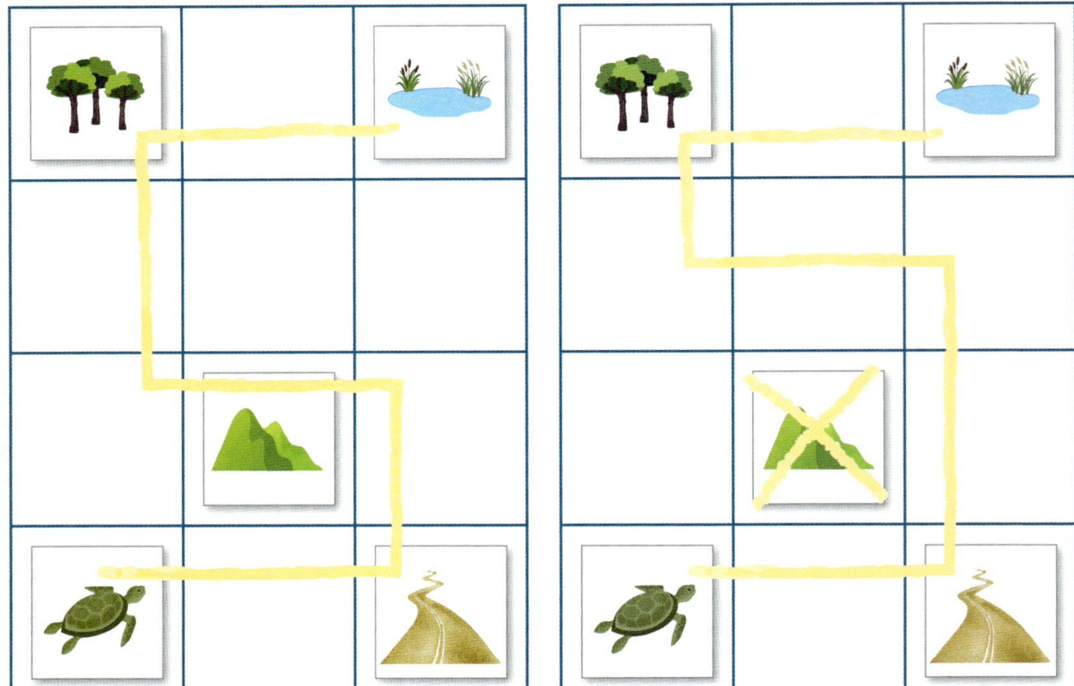

The coding grid on the left displays Hajun's original algorithm, which includes an error: the turtle going up a hill—an event that did not occur in the story. The coding grid on the right shows the corrected version of his algorithm, revised after debugging with prompting from Mx. Jimenez.

Mx. Jimenez: Yes, I see your algorithm. First, the turtle goes to the right two steps and walks along the road. (*Traces their finger to the picture card of the road.*) Second, he goes up two steps, then to the left two steps, and up one step to enter the woods. (*Drags their finger to rest on the picture card of the trees.*) Lastly, the turtle takes two steps to the right and reaches the pond. (*Brings their finger to the picture card of the pond.*) He jumps right in and has a nice, cool swim on that hot day. Well done, Hajun!

Loop

As touched on in previous chapters, a *loop* or *looping* refers to repeating a set of instructions or steps multiple times until a certain condition is met. A loop can consist of one repeated step or several repeated steps. This is a great term to introduce when children recognize patterns in a story. For instance, children might notice recurring phrases, events, actions, or themes while reading a story, which can be likened to the concept of loops. Later, this understanding can extend to coding stories on a grid, where an algorithm's sequence repeats. In other words, to "loop a sequence three times" means executing the same series of moves or actions three times in succession.

Figure 4.11 An Algorithm with Several Looping Steps

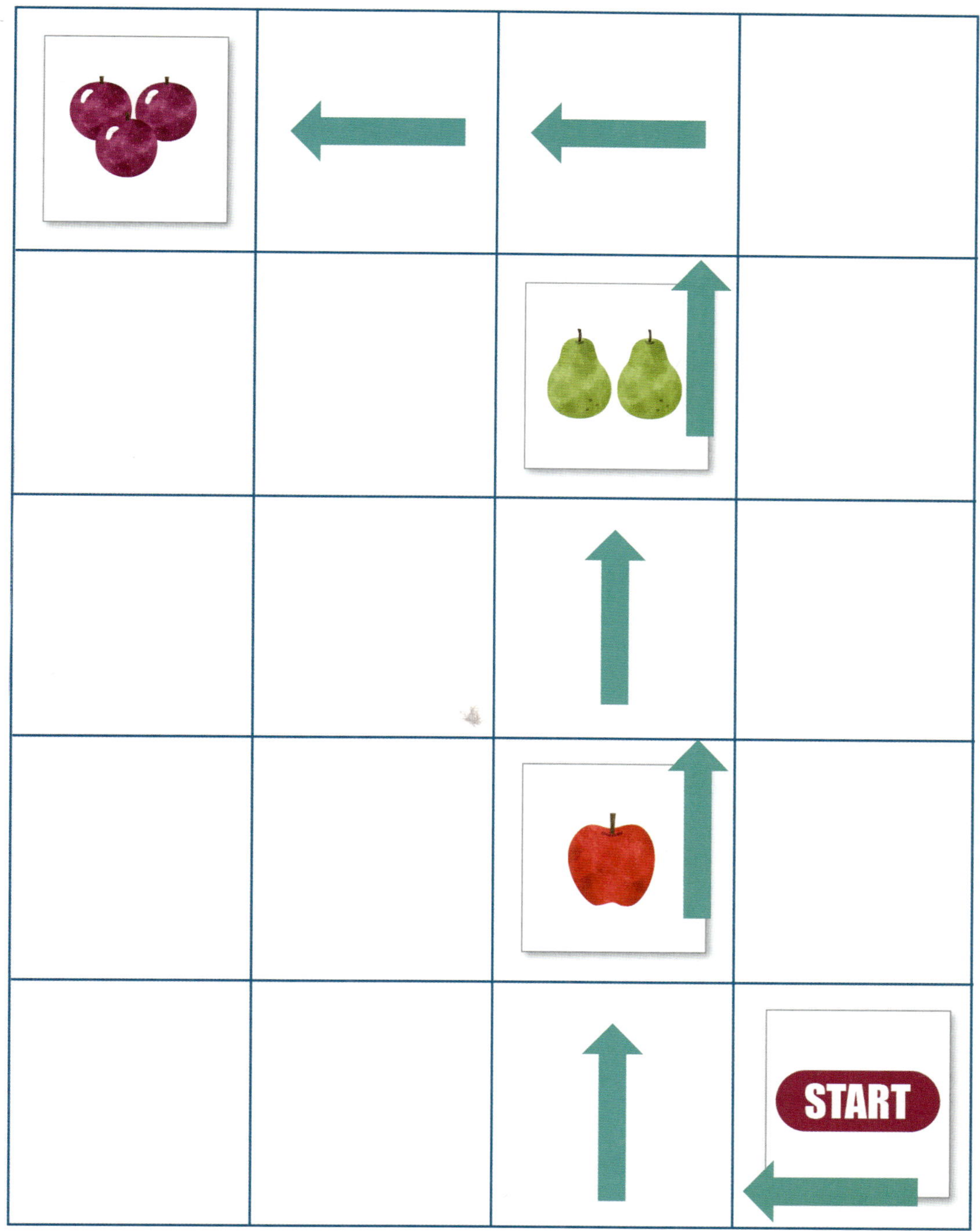

Two Children Recognize and Discuss the Loop in Their Algorithm

Ms. Viola walks around her preschool learning setting as the children work in pairs to code a story on five-by-four grids. Specifically, they are creating algorithms for what the caterpillar ate on Monday, Tuesday, and Wednesday in *The Very Hungry Caterpillar,* by Eric Carle. While observing and making notes about the children's work, she occasionally intervenes to ask a question to get some pairs thinking about how to develop a more efficient algorithm or to facilitate when other pairs seem more frustrated than productively challenged. As she pauses to listen in on a conversation between two children, Luke and Omer, she is delighted to hear them recognize a repeated pattern in some of their algorithm's steps and use terminology she explained and modeled in previous discussions.

Luke: We gotta start here. (*Points to the start square and places the caterpillar figurine on the indicated square; see Figure 4.11.*)

Omer: (*Nods.*)

Luke: The caterpillar ate the apple first. The apple is right there! (*Points to the picture card of one apple.*) Caterpillar goes this way. (*Puts down two arrow cards, the first pointing left and the second pointing up. Moves the caterpillar one step to the left and then one step up.*) Now this way for pears. (*Puts down two arrow cards, both pointing up.*) Up one, two. (*Moves the caterpillar two steps up.)*

Omer: Yes, we go up, up, up!

Luke: Mhmm. Now up one, and then two more this way for plums. (*Puts down three arrow cards, the first pointing up and the second and third both pointing left. Moves the caterpillar three steps accordingly.*) We did it!

Omer: (*Studies the grid.*) One and one and one and one. See? (*Taps on each square from the one beneath the picture card of one apple to the square with the picture card of two pears.*)

Luke: One step up four times. Oh—four loops! (*Laughs excitedly.*)

Omer: Four loops! (*Repeats and claps.*)

Ideas for Extending This Learning Experience

As children become familiar and comfortable with coding stories in the ways already explored in this chapter, this learning experience can be extended with the introduction of new methods and materials. These approaches offer opportunities for deeper engagement and additional challenges, including some intentional integration of technology. The following ideas are designed to enhance children's understanding of coding concepts while actively practicing the major computational thinking skills.

Figure 4.12 Example of a Local Map and Its Re-Creation on a Coding Grid

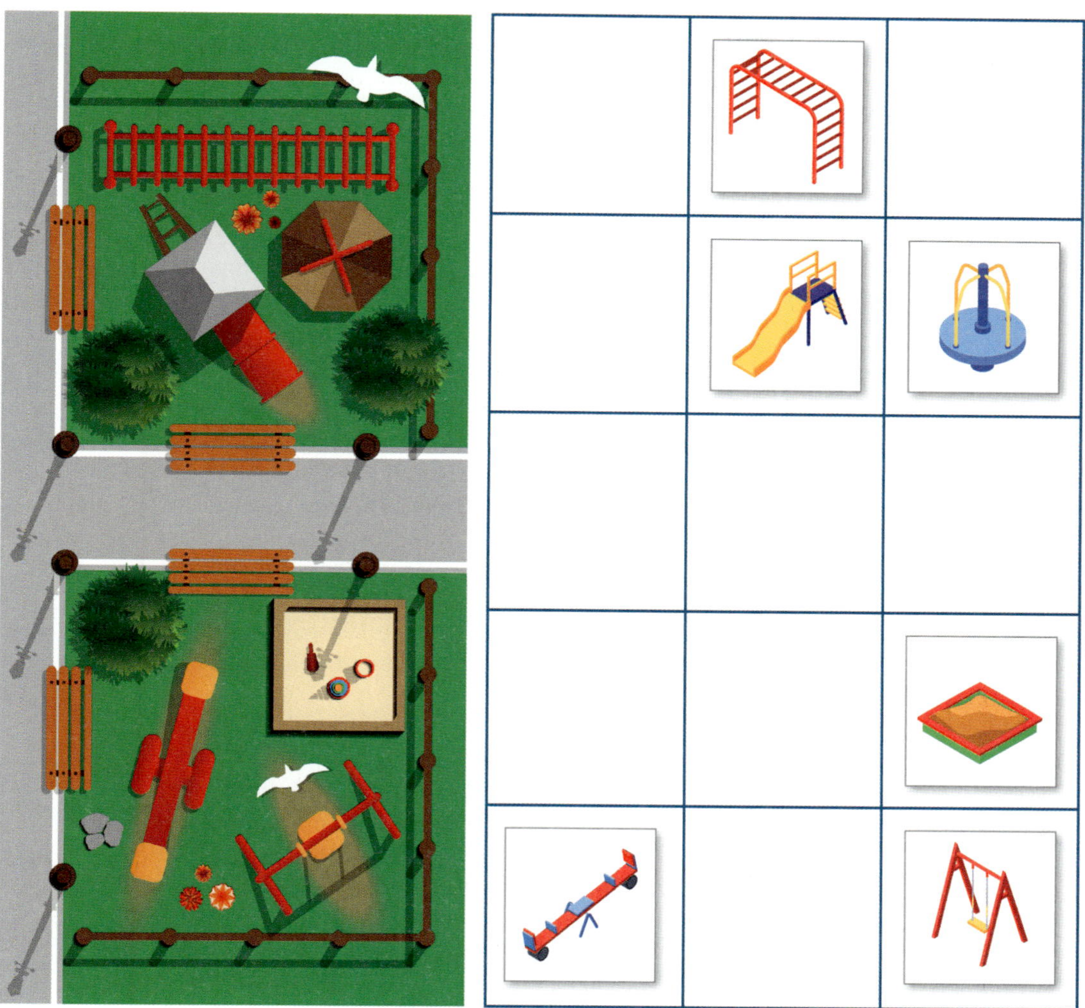

Local Maps

Using maps of familiar spaces in the community as part of children's play and learning brings coding into a real-world context that provides deeper meaning. Teachers can help children design or re-create a map within a coding grid to represent a local place they visit often, such as a grocery store, library, or park. (See Figure 4.12.) These maps can be designed on standard-size paper or as life-sized grids for the children to navigate with their bodies. Children might take turns navigating the map as themself or even as another member of the community (e.g., a family member, a delivery truck driver, a dog walker) and follow algorithms created by their peers to move between locations. This experience is a natural progression from the "I'm a Robot and I'm a Programmer" activity in Chapter 3, enhancing spatial awareness and planning through whole-body physical interaction.

To increase the challenge of this learning experience, teachers might

- Introduce visual or physical obstacles, such as construction cones, traffic signals, and stuffed animals. These require children to adjust their algorithms, encouraging them to think critically and creatively about alternative paths.
- Incorporate team-based problem solving. Divide the children into small teams and challenge them to collaboratively design the most efficient algorithm to navigate the grid (i.e., the pathway that uses the fewest steps). This promotes teamwork, communication, and logical reasoning as children compare ideas and decide on the best path to reach the end goal while considering constraints like time or movement efficiency.
- Include conditions and tools for more dynamic algorithm design. For example, a playful rule like "If the postal worker steps onto a square with a stop sign, they must wait for five seconds" can be enforced by another child playing the role of a traffic officer and keeping time with a stopwatch or sand timer. Conditions like these mimic programming logic, allowing children to explore how actions can be influenced by specific rules or triggers, fostering a deeper understanding of how algorithms or rules impact outcomes.

Programmable Robots

Programmable robots (e.g., Bee-Bots, Botley, Colby) provide an opportunity for children to revisit and build on the coding concepts they have already explored with unplugged materials in a more interactive and dynamic way. These robots enable children to direct their movements using directional arrow buttons. (See Figure 4.13.) Instead of tracing the path of an algorithm on a coding grid with their finger, a marker, or character figurine, children program the robot to follow a route with programmed commands. Programmable robots serve as a great tool when transitioning children from unplugged to plugged learning experiences because the technology requires physical manipulation of the command buttons to be directed and operated.

Provide children with materials like blank grids, markers, and props (e.g., toy buildings, trees, rocks) and encourage them to design complex paths for the robot to navigate. Children can place items on the grid to create specific obstacles and challenges, such as navigating through a maze, avoiding lava, or collecting items in a specific sequence. This not only fosters creativity and ownership but also enhances their ability to think critically about planning and sequencing.

Teachers can also organize small group activities where children take turns programming and debugging the robot. One child can input an initial code while others observe and provide feedback. If the robot encounters an error or gets stuck, the group can work together to debug the algorithm and find a solution. This collaborative approach helps children develop communication and problem-solving skills while reinforcing their understanding of coding processes like debugging and iteration.

Figure 4.13 A Programmable Robot Navigating a Coding Grid Maze

Block-Based Coding Programs

Block-based coding programs offer another accessible, engaging way for young children to explore foundational CT skills (Lee, Yunus, & Lee 2025). These plugged tools use visual—and often, tangible—interfaces that help children develop programming logic without needing to read or write traditional code. By physically or digitally manipulating blocks that represent code instructions, children explore core concepts like sequencing, cause-and-effect reasoning, debugging, and algorithmic thinking.

For example, KIBO introduces coding through physical wooden blocks that are labeled with commands (e.g., move forward, move backward, spin) and direct the actions of a programmable robot. Children arrange these blocks to form a series of actions. Then, they scan the barcode on each block in sequence using the barcode scanner built into the KIBO robot, allowing the robot to "read" the instructions they are being given. When children press the button to run their program, the robot carries out their instructions, reinforcing step-by-step problem solving and immediate feedback. Similarly, programs like Osmo and Kodable offer digital block-based experiences. Osmo uses physical coding blocks that transfer commands to a tablet, while Kodable features a drag-and-drop interface through their screen-based platform. In both, children build simple algorithms to move characters or trigger events.

With the latter two programs in particular, the focus can be shifted to interactive storytelling, child-led experimentation, and creative ownership. To implement this, teachers can invite children to design their own stories using a blank coding grid and picture cards or self-drawn images. Children select characters, settings, and events, and then plan the corresponding sequence of movements for a programmable character. Once their story is complete, children can translate it into a coded algorithm using a block-based coding program to mirror the narrative's actions. This hands-on, storytelling-to-coding approach blends narrative construction with programming logic, emphasizing creativity, planning, and testing. As children actively refine their sequences and make adjustments, they build confidence in both expressive storytelling and foundational CT skills, guided by intentional adult support when needed.

Conclusion

Coding can be a powerful tool to nurture young children's computational thinking skills, but its abstract nature makes it less likely to be incorporated in the early childhood education setting. Using stories as a framework for coding offers a playful and developmentally appropriate way to foster CT skills and coding concepts together. Coding encompasses all four of the major CT skills, and story-based coding naturally engages children in breaking down problems into manageable steps, recognizing patterns, focusing on key information, designing algorithms, and refining solutions through debugging. By scaffolding children's coding through stories, embedding CT terminology in interactions, and extending this learning experience through additional unplugged and plugged approaches, teachers provide meaningful and accessible ways for children to explore CT. These experiences build a strong foundation for future learning, equipping children with the creativity and problem-solving skills needed to navigate increasingly complex challenges.

CHAPTER 5

What's Next? Calls to Action for Educators

Thought Questions

- What strategies can teachers use to grow professionally in computational thinking?
- How can you engage children's families and the broader community to support computational thinking?
- How can teachers advocate for computational thinking?

Children are more likely to reach their full potential when they are supported by all their spheres of influence—namely, their home, their school, and their community (Epstein et al. 2019). With this understanding as the foundation, this final chapter presents a clear and actionable framework for early childhood educators to effectively integrate computational thinking into the early learning setting through three prongs:

- The first focuses on how teachers can commit to this goal in their own work and empower themselves as reflective practitioners who actively refine their teaching practices and expand their professional expertise.
- The second emphasizes building partnerships with children's families and engaging the broader local community.
- The third and last highlights the importance of advocating for CT in the early childhood education field by working collaboratively with administrators and policymakers to prioritize and support its implementation.

Every step, no matter how small, contributes to making CT an enduring and transformative part of early childhood education. Teachers, families, community members, administrators, and policymakers can leverage the roles they play in young children's lives to better equip them for the future by fostering their CT development—together.

Keep Learning and Growing

The first call to action invites you—the teacher—to focus on yourself as an early childhood educator. This section breaks down how to actualize this commitment into two distinct categories: practicing effective strategies and seeking out professional development. With consistent efforts to refine teaching strategies and explore new approaches, teachers stay current and responsive to the needs of children. Seeking professional development, on the other hand, enables teachers to expand their knowledge, deepen their expertise, and engage with a community of peers in the field. Together, these efforts ensure that teachers remain lifelong learners dedicated to enhancing teaching practices while creating rich learning experiences for the children they serve.

Practice Effective Strategies

Educators can ensure that CT becomes a meaningful and sustainable part of their early learning settings by incorporating a number of practical steps into their teaching practices. These efforts will inspire young learners to think critically, approach problems creatively, and develop the confidence and curiosity they need to navigate the complexities of the future. At the same time, they help educators deepen their own understanding of CT and become more purposeful in integrating it into everyday learning. As teachers continuously seek effective and data-driven strategies to implement CT learning experiences, they gain insights into how children interact with CT, its major skills, and its underlying concepts throughout daily routines and activities. This, in turn, helps teachers refine their pedagogical approaches to better meet the needs of the children they teach and ensure that CT moves beyond theoretical concepts to become a living, integral part of daily learning.

Identify Existing Opportunities for Computational Thinking

As explored in Chapter 3, many of the practices and routines already happening in the early learning setting (e.g., organizing materials, following step-by-step instructions, sorting objects by attributes) naturally incorporate CT concepts. Recognizing this, a good first step on the journey of integrating CT is to carefully analyze the learning experiences and activities currently in place and to identify how they align with CT skills. By being mindful of what you do as a teacher and how CT is being fostered, you can purposefully highlight and expand these learning opportunities to make CT more explicit and meaningful for children. Moreover, starting with familiar learning experiences and routines ensures that the introduction of CT feels natural and accessible for both teachers and children. This approach not only builds confidence in teaching CT, it also reinforces the idea that CT is not limited to technology-based activities—it is a versatile and integral part of everyday learning and life. Identifying these embedded CT elements additionally provides teachers with a foundation for introducing new CT learning experiences to young children and insights for building up their CT skills more intentionally.

Be Innovative When Designing and Adapting Learning Experiences

As educators of young children, it is essential to embrace creativity when teaching any new concept, and CT is no different. The ideas presented in this book provide some ways to incorporate CT in the early learning setting; however, it is important to recognize that they are only a starting point. Aside from children's families, teachers know the children they teach best. They understand children's developmental levels, interests, and needs, taking into account their social and cultural contexts. Consequently, you are uniquely positioned to understand what strategies and learning experiences are the most effective for the specific children in your early learning setting. When leveraging the learning experiences suggested in this book, teachers are encouraged to adapt, individualize, and expand on them in ways that will make the concepts they teach more relevant and engaging for the children (NAEYC 2020). This ensures that each child's learning is both meaningful and tailored to the unique dynamics of their early learning setting, which fosters engagement, curiosity, and a deeper understanding of CT concepts.

As educators of young children, it is essential to embrace creativity when teaching any new concept, and CT is no different.

Use New Tools

Exploring and integrating new tools—whether technology based or not—in the early learning setting opens up opportunities for excitement, innovation, and meaningful learning. This mindset extends to both the tools that children use directly and those primarily used by teachers to support children's learning. As emphasized throughout this book, for preschoolers, it is important to focus on tools that introduce foundational computational thinking concepts through playful, hands-on interaction. While unplugged learning experiences and tools best fit the learning needs of children in this age range, vetting and introducing select technology-based tools can also be developmentally appropriate when done with intentional guidance. For example, digital storytelling apps like ScratchJr or Seesaw allow young children to engage with basic coding principles by using sequencing commands to animate characters and create stories. Any tool provided for children to engage with should blend creativity and problem solving in accessible and fun ways.

This willingness to use new tools also extends to teachers. If children are expected to learn to manipulate a tool, teachers must be adept at using that same tool themselves. Additionally, there are teaching tools (e.g., reflection journals, interactive whiteboards) that are primarily, if not solely, used by educators as they help children learn. While trying new tools may feel unfamiliar or challenging at first, it offers a valuable opportunity for both teachers and children to grow and learn together. Experimentation allows teachers to explore various approaches, identify what resonates most with the children they teach, and individualize learning experiences to better align with the children's developmental needs and interests. This openness to innovation fosters a dynamic and inclusive learning environment where CT becomes a natural and enjoyable part of early childhood education.

Observe and Listen to Children

Teachers can learn a lot by paying close attention to how children engage with CT learning experiences. Are they actively participating and showing enthusiasm, or are they disengaged? Are they appropriately challenged, demonstrating persistence and problem solving, or do they seem confused? Observing these cues will help you understand if the learning experiences align with children's developmental levels and interests, or if they require modifications to better meet the children where they are. Based on what you see and hear, change the learning experiences accordingly. Teachers can make necessary modifications, such as simplifying tasks, providing additional support, or increasing complexity to sustain engagement and learning. For example, when sequencing a series of steps using picture cards, teachers can reduce the number of picture cards for children who are just beginning or struggling with this task, and they can increase the number of picture cards for children who regularly finish this task quickly and correctly. Regularly observing and listening to children ensures that CT activities remain effective and meaningful for all learners.

Keep a Reflection Journal

Regularly self-evaluating the effectiveness of CT learning experiences is crucial for continuous improvement of teaching practices and strategies. One way to do this is by maintaining a journal to record observations and thoughts. After each CT learning experience, take a few moments to jot down what worked well and what challenges arose. For example, you might note which elements of the learning experience engaged children the most—was it the hands-on aspect, the storytelling component, or the collaborative opportunities? Also, document any difficulties children faced, such as confusion with instructions, frustration with a task, or lack of engagement.

In addition to recording successes and challenges, a reflection journal can be used to brainstorm ideas for improvement. For instance, if children struggle with using directional language (e.g., *forward, backward, left, right*) during a movement activity, you might consider how the learning experience could be adapted. Perhaps adding visual aids with arrows, modeling the directions with the whole group, breaking the task into smaller steps, or incorporating familiar routines that involve directions (e.g., lining up, setting the table, cleaning up materials) would help make the task more meaningful next time. Conversely, if a learning experience was highly successful, reflect on why it worked and how those elements could be incorporated in the future.

A journal also serves as a repository for long-term reflections, enabling teachers to self-evaluate their teaching practices over time. For example, teachers can review their entries to track trends, such as which types of learning experiences consistently engage children or which require additional supports. By regularly updating the journal and revisiting past entries, teachers can refine their practices, ensure that CT learning experiences remain aligned with children's developmental needs, and build a repertoire of effective strategies that evolve alongside the children's growth and interests.

Conduct and Share Peer Observations

Peer evaluation is another key component in making teaching more effective and impactful. The absence of hierarchy between peers encourages informal, spontaneous, and transparent discussions. By engaging in reciprocal peer observations, teachers can gain valuable insights into their implementation of CT and offer the same in turn. If possible, colleagues can sit in during CT learning experiences to later provide feedback, identify strengths, and pinpoint areas for improvement (Recchia & Puig 2018). However, considering the busy schedules of teachers, it may be more feasible to record yourself teaching children CT concepts and engaging children in learning experiences that can then be shared with colleagues. This allows peers to observe and provide feedback at their convenience, minimizing disruption to their routines.

Teachers can work together in advance to outline specific questions they would like peers to focus on when conducting their observations (e.g., Do the learning experiences align with children's developmental level? How are CT concepts integrated in play and daily routines? In what ways are children actively engaged?) or leave it to the observer to tailor the feedback. Shared reflection logs—whether digital or physical—offer a space for teachers to leave feedback and respond to one another asynchronously or during in-person meetings. By leveraging these methods, teachers create a culture of improvement and collaboration.

Improve Through Professional Development

To grow professionally, it is essential for teachers to proactively seek out opportunities to enhance their knowledge about computational thinking. Although CT has been present in early childhood education for some time, its formal recognition as an emergent concept in this field is relatively recent. This growing awareness has led to an increase in research exploring effective pedagogies to support and promote CT development in young learners. So that CT learning experiences provided to children remain playful, engaging, and developmentally appropriate, teachers must engage in continuous learning to stay informed about these evolving studies and practices.

Attend Conferences and Workshops

Participating in conferences and workshops focused on early learning and CT integration provides teachers with opportunities to grow professionally and stay informed about the latest advancements in the field. These events often feature expert speakers who share cutting-edge research and innovative strategies for implementing CT in the classroom. For instance, informational seminars might delve into topics like play-based approaches to coding or the role of CT in fostering critical thinking in young learners. Meanwhile, interactive workshops or breakout sessions allow teachers to experience firsthand hands-on activities, such as building simple algorithms with tactile materials or exploring unplugged CT games. These forums not only deepen theoretical understanding but provide actionable ideas to bring back to the early learning setting. Additionally, conferences frequently feature exhibitors that showcase new resources and tools, helping teachers identify and stay ahead of emerging trends.

Beyond sessions, conferences and workshops create a collaborative environment where educators can network with peers, mentors, and industry leaders (Vujičić & Čamber Tambolaš 2017). Teachers can exchange ideas, discuss challenges, and share successes with others who are equally passionate about early learning and CT. This sense of community fosters ongoing partnership and inspires teachers to refine their practices and adopt new strategies. Through these events, teachers not only enhance their pedagogical knowledge of CT, they gain the confidence to advocate for CT integration within their settings, programs, and communities.

Seek Out Certifications and Other Resources

To enhance your understanding and implementation of CT, explore resources designed specifically for early childhood educators. These might include certifications, microcredentials, tutorials, online toolkits, lesson plans, and much more. Training-oriented resources might be held in person, virtually, or some combination of both. While some of these supports might have associated costs, a number of them are made available for free. Here are a few organizations you can begin with:

- Code.org (www.code.org) offers a wide range of free resources, from materials for teachers (e.g., lesson plans, slide decks, assessments) to tools for learners to engage with directly (e.g., videos, activities, tutorials). While it is aimed at education in kindergarten through 12th grade, many of its offerings are also appropriate for preschoolers.
- Digital Promise (www.digitalpromise.org) provides a mix of no-cost and low-cost microcredentials focused on specific skills and competencies, including computational thinking.
- The International Society for Technology in Education (ISTE; www.iste.org) empowers educators to reimagine and redesign learning through pedagogy and intentional use of technology. Its CT-related resources and services include books, video tutorials, and webinars.

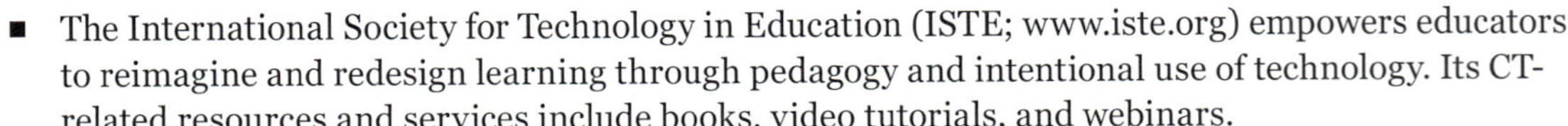

Form Professional Relationships

Connecting and collaborating with fellow early childhood educators provides invaluable opportunities for professional growth. Learning with and from others in your field often brings to light unique perspectives and creative solutions to common challenges, such as adapting CT concepts for different age groups or embedding CT into everyday routines (Recchia & Puig 2018; Thornton & Cherrington 2018). These professional relationships can take shape in a variety of ways. You might work with a more experienced educator as your mentor in a one-on-one capacity. Based on their own expertise, mentors can give feedback about your teaching practices, offer advice about strategies, and provide ideas for you to use in the early learning setting (LeeKeenan & Ponte 2018). Observing experienced educators in action also allows teachers to see CT concepts being effectively implemented while concurrently balancing considerations like classroom management and engaging diverse learners. Teachers can refine their own practices by reflecting on these observations, asking questions, and discussing outcomes.

Alternately—or additionally—you can connect with peers to exchange ideas, share experiences, and discuss strategies for integrating CT. These collaborative learning relationships can be fostered through formal or informal means. They could include joining a professional learning community, a local early childhood education network, or a national professional organization. There are also online forums, such as EDUCAUSE Community Groups (www.educause.edu/community) and HELLO (https://hello.NAEYC.org), where educators can connect with each other to ask and answer questions, suggest and find resources, and more. Professional relationships with fellow educators not only strengthen individual teaching strategies but also foster a collective commitment to innovation and continuous improvement in CT education for young children.

Create Opportunities for Education and Connection

By engaging with children's families and members of the local community, teachers can create opportunities to extend computational thinking beyond the early learning setting. Such partnerships not only enhance families' and community members' understanding of the importance of CT, they empower these individuals to actively nurture these skills. Through collaborative initiatives like the ones explored here, teachers, families, and communities foster environments where CT development is integrated into everyday experiences, reinforces CT's relevance and impact on children's growth, and helps children develop the foundational skills needed to thrive in a digital society.

Partner with Families

Families are children's first teachers. They are a rich source of insight into what excites and motivates their children, such as favorite hobbies, traditions, and routines (Cohen & Anders 2019). By partnering with families to understand the funds of knowledge that children bring with them into the early learning setting, educators can make children's learning—including CT learning—more meaningful and relevant (NAEYC 2020). When teachers and families work together to create environments that respect and nurture children's CT development, children's ability to transfer knowledge gained in one context and creatively apply it in another is enhanced.

By partnering with families to understand the funds of knowledge that children bring with them into the early learning setting, educators can make children's learning—including CT learning—more meaningful and relevant.

Share Instances of CT Happening in the Early Learning Setting

Ongoing communication with families helps build understanding and trust while encouraging families to try similar learning experiences at home (Graham-Clay 2024). Weekly updates through newsletters, emails, texts, or blog posts can describe what CT is and why it is important for children to develop it. Alongside brief explanations of the skills and concepts children are learning, providing visual media allows families to see this learning in action. For example, you can share photos of children creating bead patterns, audio clips of children explaining how they solved a puzzle, or brief videos of children building structures with blocks. All of these showcase for families the practical applications of CT and illustrate how their child's thinking contributed to the outcome.

Throughout these communications, it's important to emphasize how CT supports children's holistic development and learning. Explain how solving puzzles not only enhances children's CT skills, it also supports their cognitive development. Describe that creating patterns fosters both CT and creativity. Highlight how group projects build problem-solving skills through CT while also encouraging teamwork. By clearly articulating the connection between CT and all other aspects of children's development and learning, educators can help families to view CT skills as an integrated part of their child's growth rather than a separate area of learning.

Host a Family CT Day

Holding a dedicated event for families about computational thinking, such as Family CT Day, provides an engaging and interactive forum for them to learn about CT and its importance in early childhood and beyond. Ideally, this event takes place in person. However, to make it accessible to families who may be unable to join because of conflicts, consider recording the event and making it available for later viewing or even streaming it live on a closed online platform. The specifics of the event will be informed by your goals in holding it and individualized to meet children's families where they are, but the following are some suggestions you might incorporate. Begin with an introduction to or refresher about CT and the major skills and concepts it encompasses, highlighting how these skills and concepts support creative thinking and efficient problem solving in young children. With this foundation set, guide families to engage with their children in hands-on CT learning experiences, such as building simple structures with straws or exploring how to code a story. If interest and time permit, you might host this event several times throughout the year (e.g., quarterly) with a unique theme for each to provide focus and variety (e.g., Exploring Algorithms in Everyday Life). Feedback forms give families a way to share their thoughts on the event and inform the planning of subsequent events.

Encourage Families to Explore CT at Home

Children benefit when CT skills learned in the early learning setting are reinforced in the home context. Teachers can provide families with materials and resources that encourage CT learning experiences at home. These might include informational booklets, links to websites and apps, and one-sheets with practical and accessible ideas for integrating CT practice into their daily activities with children. That last resource can be especially helpful when it highlights things families already do with their children and how it naturally involves computational thinking. For instance, point out how families can gamify and use CT terms to talk about chores like cleaning up toys, sorting laundry, and organizing groceries by attributes like color, shape, size, or type. These tasks foster categorization, pattern recognition, and logical thinking. Families can also guide children in creating step-by-step instructions (algorithms) for tasks like setting and clearing the table or routines like brushing teeth. This helps children break familiar processes into manageable steps and practice sequencing skills.

To extend these practices, families might also be encouraged to embed CT learning through all-new activities. For example, if their child enjoys cooking and baking with them, they might design a family cookbook together, with children helping to create sequential recipes that outline the steps for their favorite meals. This not only builds CT skills but also strengthens family connections and integrates cultural or personal traditions associated with family food. Playing games that encourage pattern recognition and problem solving, such as puzzles, matching games, or even simple board games, further supports CT development in a fun and interactive way. These activities provide families with practical tools to engage their children in CT practices while reinforcing the connection between home and school.

Invite Families to Codesign CT Learning Experiences

Asking families to help codesign CT learning experiences helps to ensure that children's learning is engaging, relevant, and meaningful. Educators can gather input from families through surveys, suggestion boxes, or casual conversations to learn about their ideas, which may be informed by their daily routines, cultural traditions, and values. Hosting brainstorming workshops or family engagement nights provides another venue for families to offer and discuss suggestions. For example, a family that enjoys games such as mancala or dominoes might propose incorporating these in the early learning setting to foster CT concepts like pattern recognition, sequencing, and strategic problem solving. Similarly, a family's traditional dance or custom might inspire activities such as creating algorithms by mapping out the steps involved. By incorporating family input at this level, teachers and families continue to reinforce the bridge between home and school that enriches children's learning. When families see their knowledge, perspectives, and practices valued and reflected in the early learning setting, they feel more connected to their child's education. CT learning experiences that teach essential skills while also resonating deeply with children's lived experiences make learning more impactful and enjoyable (Hubelbank et al. 2024).

Empower Families to Be CT Advocates

Families can be powerful allies in promoting CT. Though some family members may not recognize their potential in this role, educators can step in to encourage and uplift their voices. As a first step, it is critical that families understand the value and importance of CT for their children's learning and future success. Educators can equip families with clear, concise information about CT, using brochures, brief presentations, short videos, and real-world examples to demonstrate its relevance and benefits. Many of the strategies already discussed in this section also serve as effective vehicles to share this information and help them become enthusiastic supporters. Advocacy kits containing tips for incorporating CT into daily life, a glossary of key terms, and practical examples of learning experiences can further support their efforts.

By providing families with the information and tools they need, you build their knowledge and confidence as advocates. From there, their advocacy can happen in many different ways. They might organize or support funding initiatives and resource allocations to integrate CT in the early learning program. Families can also participate in community advocacy efforts, such as attending community board meetings, joining parent-teacher associations, or collaborating with local organizations to advance the inclusion of CT in early childhood education. Families can also inspire others by sharing their success stories through social media, local events, or family networks. By promoting equitable access to CT learning opportunities, families help ensure that all children can benefit from these essential skills, creating a broader and lasting impact.

Involve the Community

Engaging the broader community in CT initiatives can significantly enhance early learning experiences for children. While educators and families play a central role in supporting young learners, involving other community members, organizations, and local leaders helps build a well-rounded ecosystem that values and promotes CT. By working together, educators and the community can enhance a shared understanding of the importance of CT, ensuring all children have access to high-quality CT learning experiences.

Partner with Organizations and Institutions

Collaborating with local organizations and institutions that serve the community, such as libraries and children's museums, can lead to wider-reaching CT learning opportunities for the children you teach and the community at large. For example, with an organization's resources, you might organize more expansive CT-focused events with hands-on activities, story time sessions, and interactive exhibits. Additionally, showcasing documentation of children's CT learning experiences in public community spaces like community centers brings computational thinking to the attention of neighbors and others who might not be familiar with it, which can foster further interest and discussions on the topic (Helm, Katz, & Wilson 2023).

Build Connections with Local Businesses and Industries

Reaching out to network with local businesses and industries can lead to valuable resources, expertise, and advocacy opportunities to support the integration of CT in early childhood education. One potential starting point is engaging with your local chamber of commerce to share your goals and ideas for partnership with their members. For example, you might invite a technician from the local electronics repair shop or a professional from a field like computer science or robotics as a guest speaker to the early learning program to share with children (and their families, if possible) how CT skills and concepts like problem solving and sequencing are applied in their daily work. Additionally, to build name recognition, businesses might donate funds or sponsor CT tools and materials. Educators can also proactively seek funding from local community grants focused on early childhood education, CT, or STEM initiatives, providing additional resources to support these efforts. Such collaborations not only inspire children by linking CT to career paths but also engage families, helping them understand its importance. By fostering these relationships, teachers can build long-term community support for CT initiatives, ensuring young learners have meaningful opportunities to develop these essential skills.

Advocate for Computational Thinking

Advocating for computational thinking in early childhood education is essential to ensure young children have access to meaningful opportunities to develop their CT skills from the early years. Teachers play a critical role in highlighting the importance of CT and its long-term benefits to stakeholders, not just for achieving academic success but also for preparing children to navigate an increasingly digital world. By sharing their expertise and collaborating with families, community members, and local leaders, teachers can raise awareness of CT's value and drive initiatives that promote its integration into early learning environments.

Collaborate with Administrators

Collaborating with early childhood program administrators (e.g., directors, principals) is a vital aspect of teacher advocacy. Teachers can work closely with administrators to communicate the importance of CT and its role in fostering creative thinking and problem solving in young children. Through ongoing partnership with administrators, you can champion CT as an essential component of early learning, laying a strong foundation for CT education in early childhood.

Invite Administrators to Observe the Class

If administrators are not familiar with computational thinking or do not know what it looks like in practice, invite them to observe your early learning setting to help them understand its educational value. Observing children engaged in hands-on, play-based CT learning provides an informative and approachable introduction to this skill set, offering a firsthand perspective on how CT is naturally integrated into early learning. For example, administrators can watch children working together to create step-by-step instructions (algorithms) for building block structures, solving puzzles, or engaging in unplugged coding activities.

Following the observation, engage in discussions with administrators about what they observed and how computational thinking was present. Teachers should prepare brief notes or summaries that outline how CT has been implemented in the early learning setting, the specific skills children have acquired, and data or examples that showcase these achievements. Additionally, explaining how CT aligns with the existing curriculum and connects to early learning standards will further emphasize its inherent relevance. For instance, teachers might point out how categorizing objects by shared attributes directly supports foundational math and critical thinking skills while also aligning with developmental goals like fostering logical reasoning and collaboration. You can also discuss how these learning experiences prepare children for more advanced STEM learning, helping administrators see the long-term benefits of CT.

By creating an open and collaborative environment, teachers can use these observational visits as a starting point for meaningful conversations about the importance of CT in early education. This approach not only helps administrators understand CT in action but also strengthens their support for integrating CT across the program or school.

Request Professional Development

Program administrators play a crucial role in supporting teachers' professional development. Many administrators already solicit teacher input and suggestions for the kind of education and training experiences in which they are interested. Make use of these opportunities—or, if they are not present, make use of one-on-one conversations or staff meetings—to highlight computational thinking as an area you would like to develop your knowledge and job skills. Some professional development strategies, such as book groups or professional learning communities, might be established at the program level at no or low cost. Others that require more substantial monetary investment (e.g., bringing in experts to provide onsite workshops, attending professional conferences) will necessitate discussion, buy-in, and consensus among administrators and colleagues on how to best use allocated funds.

When advocating for CT professional development, you can emphasize how learning more about CT helps all teachers improve in pedagogical skills across disciplines and often goes hand in hand with their other goals (Haines et al. 2019). Be prepared to share specific ideas to make your case. For example, if the administrators want all staff to be trained on how to make outdoor play more structured sometimes, you may suggest exploring how CT can be infused into outdoor activities through obstacle courses or scavenger hunts that involve sequencing, logic, and problem solving. If smoother transitions are a shared goal among staff, you could propose training on CT concepts like decomposition and algorithms to help break routines into smaller, manageable steps. Concrete examples like these show that CT professional development does more than introduce new ideas; it deepens and extends what teachers are already doing. In this way, CT-focused professional development supports program-wide goals and reinforces a culture of responsive, innovative practice that better aligns education with the evolving needs of society.

CT-focused professional development supports program-wide goals and reinforces a culture of responsive, innovative practice that better aligns education with the evolving needs of society.

Engage with Policymakers

Policymakers shape educational priorities, allocate funding, and establish learning standards that directly impact classroom practice. While they may seem distant from day-to-day teaching, there are a number of ways teachers can share the experiences and practical knowledge they possess to inform and influence the policies they enact. By engaging with policymakers at the local, state, or national level, teachers can help ensure that CT is recognized as an essential skill that deserves to be embedded into early childhood education standards, supported by resources, and included in long-term planning.

Be Informed

Being an effective advocate means being an informed advocate. To confidently speak up for CT and early childhood education, teachers need to understand the broader policy landscape and know when decisions are being made (NAEYC 2025). Join early childhood education associations, advocacy networks, or STEM coalitions that provide timely updates on education policy, legislative proposals, and funding opportunities. Many of these organizations also offer webinars, newsletters, and action alerts that break down complex policies into digestible summaries. Stay connected to reliable sources, such as state education agencies, local early childhood advisory councils, and national education organizations. These groups often host meetings, share policy updates, and provide opportunities for educators to lend their voice through surveys, testimony, or public comment. By remaining informed, teachers will be better positioned to act when opportunities to influence policy arise and to share classroom stories that demonstrate why CT matters in early learning.

Effectively Communicate and Present Data

Once teachers are informed and connected with advocacy networks, the next step is to share their classroom experiences and data to influence policy. Advocacy efforts might include presenting evidence during legislative sessions, participating in policy roundtables, or collaborating with professional organizations to draft recommendations for CT integration. Teachers looking to engage in these efforts can start by connecting with organizations that monitor and advocate for educational policies. Groups like NAEYC, ISTE, and state education agencies often track policy developments, offer resources, and provide guidance on advocacy, sometimes even seeking feedback directly from educators. ISTE, for example, annually hosts a robust advocacy meeting (i.e., EdTech Advocacy Day) with training resources and planned events for educators to take part in. Teachers are encouraged to be proactive in participating in various forms of advocacy efforts.

To support these efforts, teachers can offer compelling, classroom-based evidence to help policymakers understand the value of early learning. By sharing data (e.g., anecdotal notes, teaching journals, observation logs), relevant research findings, and classroom success stories, teachers illustrate the positive impact of CT on children's cognitive, social, and emotional development. Additionally, teachers can provide user-friendly reports with visuals, such as charts, graphs, and photos of children's work samples, to help policymakers better understand its impacts. For example, teachers could share metrics such as improvements in problem-solving abilities, increased collaboration among students during CT activities, or enhanced persistence when tackling challenges in the classroom. To make the case even stronger, teachers can highlight the alignment of CT with broader educational goals, such as preparing children for a technology-driven future, fostering critical thinking, and promoting equity in STEM education—all of which help build a strong argument for including CT in early childhood policy and practice.

Invite Policymakers to the Early Learning Setting

Teachers working with administrators can host visits for local policymakers (e.g., city or county council members, local education administrators, early childhood advisory council members, community education advocates) to observe CT activities in the classroom. Before reaching out, it is essential to research their background, educational interests, and priorities, especially their views on early childhood education and STEM. This allows teachers to align their intended message with the policymaker's specific educational vision. In turn, these visits allow policymakers to see CT in action and witness its benefits firsthand. In addition to observing, you might consider inviting them to engage with children during a learning experience or participate in a short discussion with teachers about how CT supports broader learning goals, such as problem solving, collaboration, and language development. To maximize impact, prepare brief explanations of the learning goals and examples of children's thinking or work samples. Even a short visit can leave a lasting impression and help build support for CT in early education policy and funding decisions.

Conclusion

The journey to integrating computational thinking into early learning settings requires a combination of thoughtful reflection and deliberate action. Part of the reflective thinking process involves seeing CT as more than just a set of skills—it is a transformative mindset that prepares children to approach real-world challenges and solve problems with confidence, creativity, and resilience. Teachers hold the power to shape the broader educational landscape by committing to learning and growing in their own practice and working with colleagues, families, local communities, and policymakers. Through these efforts, teachers can amplify the importance of CT to all stakeholders of early childhood education, building awareness of its importance and support for its integration. Educators create dynamic and inclusive classrooms where CT empowers young learners to become creative thinkers and effective problem solvers who will thrive in a digital world.

References

Baroody, A.J. 2017. "The Use of Concrete Experiences in Early Childhood Mathematics Instruction." In *The Development of Early Childhood Mathematics Education,* eds. J. Sarama, D.H. Clements, C. Germeroth, & C. Day-Hess, 43–94. Vol. 53 of *Advances in Child Development and Behavior*, ed. J. Benson. Academic Press.

Barr, V., & C. Stephenson. 2011. "Bringing Computational Thinking to K–12: What Is Involved and What Is the Role of the Computer Science Education Community?" *ACM Inroads* 2 (1): 48–54.

Barron, B. 2000. "Achieving Coordination in Collaborative Problem-Solving Groups." *The Journal of the Learning Sciences* 9 (4): 403–36.

Berk, L.E., & A.B. Meyers. 2013. "The Role of Make-Believe Play in the Development of Executive Function: Status of Research and Future Directions." *American Journal of Play* 6 (1): 98–110.

Bers, M.U. 2021. *Coding as a Playground: Programming and Computational Thinking in the Early Childhood Classroom*. 2nd ed. Routledge.

Bers, M.U., L. Flannery, E.R. Kazakoff, & A. Sullivan. 2014. "Computational Thinking and Tinkering: Exploration of an Early Childhood Robotics Curriculum." *Computers & Education* 72: 145–57.

Bers, M.U., C. González-González, & M.B. Armas–Torres. 2019. "Coding as a Playground: Promoting Positive Learning Experiences in Childhood Classrooms." *Computers & Education* 138: 130–45.

Bishop, R.S. 1990. "Mirrors, Windows, and Sliding Glass Doors." *Perspectives* 6 (3): ix–xi.

Brennan, K., & M. Resnick. 2012. "New Frameworks for Studying and Assessing the Development of Computational Thinking." Paper presented at the annual meeting of the American Educational Research Association, in Vancouver, BC, Canada. http://scratched.gse.harvard.edu/ct/files/AERA2012.pdf.

Brooks, M. 2009. "Drawing, Visualization, and Young Children's Exploration of 'Big Ideas.'" *International Journal of Science Education* 31 (3): 319–41.

CASEL (Collaborative for Academic, Social, and Emotional Learning). n.d. "Fundamentals of SEL." https://casel.org/fundamentals-of-sel.

Chi, M.T.H. 2000. "Self-Explaining Expository Texts: The Dual Processes of Generating Inferences and Repairing Mental Models." In *Advances in Instructional Psychology,* ed. R. Glaser, Vol. 5, 161–238. Lawrence Erlbaum Associates.

Clarke-Midura, J., D. Silvis, J.F. Shumway, V.R. Lee, & J. S. Hamilton. 2021. "Developing a Kindergarten Computational Thinking Assessment Using Evidence-Centered Design: The Case of Algorithmic Thinking." *Computer Science Education* 31 (2): 117–40.

Cohen, F., & Y. Anders. 2019. "Family Involvement in Early Childhood Education and Care and Its Effects on the Social-Emotional and Language Skills of 3-Year-Old Children." *School Effectiveness and School Improvement* 31 (1): 125–42.

Collins, M.F., & J.A. Schickedanz. 2024. *So Much More than the ABCs: The Early Phases of Reading and Writing*. Rev. ed. NAEYC.

Dale, N., & J. Lewis. 2019. *Computer Science Illuminated.* 7th ed. Jones & Bartlett Learning.

del Olmo-Muñoz, J., R. Cózar-Gutiérrez, & J.A. González-Calero. 2020. "Computational Thinking Through Unplugged Activities in Early Years of Primary Education." *Computers & Education* 150: 103832. doi:10.1016/j.compedu.2020.103832.

Epstein, J.L., M.G. Sanders, S. Sheldon, B.S. Simon, K.C. Salinas, N.R. Jansorn, F.L. VanVoorhis, C.S. Martin, B.G. Thomas, M.D. Greenfield, D.J. Hutchins, & K.J. Williams. 2019. *School, Family, and Community Partnerships: Your Handbook for Action*. 4th ed. Corwin Press.

Gathercole, S.E., & T.P. Alloway. 2008. *Working Memory and Learning: A Practical Guide for Teachers*. SAGE Publications.

Gay, G. 2018. *Culturally Responsive Teaching: Theory, Research, and Practice*. 3rd ed. Teachers College Press.

Goldin-Meadow, S. 2005. *Hearing Gesture: How Our Hands Help Us Think*. Harvard University Press.

Graham-Clay, S. 2024. "Communicating with Parents 2.0: Strategies for Teachers." *School Community Journal* 34 (1): 9–60.

Grimone-Hopkins, J., & C. Mirtes. 2024. "Planning for Individuality in Preschool Spaces." *Teaching Young Children* 17 (3): 4–7.

Grover, S., & R. Pea. 2013. "Computational Thinking in K–12: A Review of the State of the Field." *Educational Researcher* 42 (1): 38–43.

Haines, S., M. Krach, A. Pustaka, Q. Li, & L.J. Richman. 2019. "The Effects of Computational Thinking Professional Development on STEM Teachers' Perceptions and Pedagogical Practices." *Athens Journal of Sciences* 6 (2): 97–122.

Hanline, M.F., S. Milton, & P. Phelps. 2010. "The Relationship Between Preschool Block Play and Reading and Math Abilities in Early Elementary School: A Longitudinal Study of Children with and Without Disabilities." *Early Child Development and Care* 180 (8): 1005–17.

Helm, J.H., L.G. Katz, & R. Wilson. 2023. *Young Investigators: The Project Approach in the Early Years*. 4th ed. Teachers College Press.

Hemmeter, M.L, M. Ostrosky, & L. Fox. 2006. "Social and Emotional Foundations for Early Learning: A Conceptual Model for Intervention." *School Psychology Review* 35 (4): 583–601.

Hsu, T.-C., S.-C. Chang, & Y.-T. Hung. 2018. "How to Learn and How to Teach Computational Thinking: Suggestions Based on a Review of the Literature." *Computers & Education* 126: 296–310.

Hubelbank, J., M. Dubosarsky, S. Kayumova, T. Davis, N. Sann, S. Fortin, & G. Smith. 2024. "Integrating Computational Thinking Practices into Early Childhood Education in Culturally Responsive Ways: Insights from Research–Practice Partnership." *Future in Educational Research* 2 (4): 359–81.

Hynes-Berry, M., & L. Grandau. 2019. *Where's the Math? Books, Games, and Routines to Spark Children's Thinking*. NAEYC.

ISTE (International Society for Technology in Education). 2019. *ISTE Standards*. ISTE. https://iste.org/standards.

ISTE (International Society for Technology in Education) & CSTA (Computer Science Teachers Association). 2011. "Operational Definition of Computational Thinking for K–12 Education." https://cdn.iste.org/www-root/Computational_Thinking_Operational_Definition_ISTE.pdf.

Joseph, G.E., & P.S. Strain. 2003. "Helping Young Children Control Anger and Handle Disappointment." *Young Exceptional Children* 7 (1): 21–29.

Joswick, C., J. Lee, R. Jocius, & K. Pole. 2023. "Reading, Coding, and Crafting." *Young Children* 78 (4): 38–46.

Knuth, D.E. 1972. "Ancient Babylonian Algorithms." *Communications of the ACM* 15 (7): 671–77.

Kolodner, J.L., J.T. Gray, & B.B. Fasse. 2003. "Promoting Transfer Through Case-Based Reasoning: Rituals and Practices in Learning by Design Classrooms." *Cognitive Science Quarterly* 3 (2): 183–232.

Kramer, J. 2007. "Is Abstraction the Key to Computing?" *Communications of the ACM* 50 (4): 36–42.

Labadie, M., K. Pole, & R. Rogers. 2013. "How Kindergarten Students Connect and Critically Respond to Themes of Social Class in Children's Literature." *Literacy Research and Instruction* 52 (4): 312–38.

Lavigne, H., J. Orr, & M. Wolsky. 2022. "Helping Your Preschool Child with Computational Thinking." Message in a Backpack. *Teaching Young Children* 15 (3): 7.

Lee, J. 2016. *How to Teach Math to Children*. 2nd ed. Cognella Academic Publishing.

Lee, J. 2020. "Coding in Early Childhood." *Contemporary Issues in Early Childhood* 21 (3): 266–69.

Lee, J., D. Collins, & L. Winkelman. 2015. "Connecting 2-D and 3-D: Drafting Blueprints, Building, and Playing with Blocks." *Young Children* 70 (1): 32–35.

Lee, J., C. Joswick, & K. Pole. 2023. "Classroom Play and Activities to Support Computational Thinking Development in Early Childhood." *Early Childhood Education Journal* 51 (3): 457–68.

Lee, J., C. Joswick, K. Pole, & R. Jocius. 2022. "Algorithm Design for Young Children." *Contemporary Issues in Early Childhood* 23 (2): 198–202.

Lee, J., & J. Junho. 2019. "Implementing Unplugged Coding Activities in Early Childhood Classrooms." *Early Childhood Education Journal* 47 (6): 709–16.

Lee, J., S. Yunus, & J.O. Lee. 2025. "Investigating Children's Programming Skills Through Play with Robots (KIBO)." *Early Childhood Education Journal* 53 (1): 109–17.

LeeKeenan, D., & I.C. Ponte. 2018. *From Survive to Thrive: A Director's Guide for Leading an Early Childhood Program*. NAEYC.

McCormick, K.I., & J.A. Hall. 2022. "Computational Thinking Learning Experiences, Outcomes, and Research in Preschool Settings: A Scoping Review of Literature." *Education and Informational Technology* 27 (3): 3777–812.

McLennan, D.P. 2017. "Creating Coding Stories and Games." *Teaching Young Children* 10 (3): 18–21.

Morin, A.M. 2024. "10 Healthy Snacks for Kids to Make." *Parents,* July 22. www.parents.com/fun-healthy-snacks-for-kids-to-make-8663822.

Murcia, K., & K.-S. Tang. 2019. "Exploring the Multimodality of Young Children's Coding." *Australian Educational Computing* 34 (1). https://journal.acce.edu.au/index.php/AEC/article/view/208.

NAEYC. 2020. "Developmentally Appropriate Practice." Position statement. NAEYC. www.naeyc.org/resources/position-statements/dap.

NAEYC. 2022. *Developmentally Appropriate Practice in Early Childhood Programs Serving Children from Birth Through Age 8*. 4th ed. NAEYC.

NAEYC. 2025. "Building Skills and Confidence as an Early Childhood Advocate." *NAEYC* (blog), April 9. www.naeyc.org/resources/blog/building-advocacy-skills.

NCPMI (National Center for Pyramid Model Innovations). 2020. "Visual Supports for Routines, Schedules, and Transitions." Online resource, September 30. https://challengingbehavior.org/docs/Routine_cards_home.pdf.

Newcombe, N.S., & J. Huttenlocher. 2000. *Making Space: The Development of Spatial Representation and Reasoning*. MIT Press.

Ottenbreit-Leftwich, A., & A. Yadav, eds. 2021. *Computational Thinking in PreK–5: Empirical Evidence for Integration and Future Directions*. Association for Computing Machinery; Robin Hood Learning + Technology Fund. doi:10.1145/3507951.

Papadakis, S., M. Kalogiannakis, & N. Zaranis. 2016. "Developing Fundamental Programming Concepts and Computational Thinking with ScratchJr in Preschool Education: A Case Study." *International Journal of Mobile Learning and Organisation* 10 (3): 187–202.

Papert, S. 1980. *Mind Storms: Children, Computers, and Powerful Ideas*. Basic Books.

Papert, S. 1996. "An Exploration in the Space of Mathematics Educations." *International Journal of Computers for Mathematical Learning* 1: 95–123.

Partnership for 21st Century Skills. 2009. "P21 Framework Definitions." https://files.eric.ed.gov/fulltext/ED519462.pdf.

Perlis, A., & C. Thornton. 1960. "Symbol Manipulation by Threaded Lists." *Communications of the ACM* 3 (4): 195–204.

Piaget, J. 1952. *The Origins of Intelligence in Children*. Trans. M. Cook. International Universities Press.

Pila, S., F. Aladé, K.J. Sheehan, A.R. Lauricella, & E.A. Wartella. 2019. "Learning to Code Via Tablet Applications: An Evaluation of *Daisy the Dinosaur* and *Kodable* as Learning Tools for Young Children." *Computers & Education* 128: 52–62.

Qu, J.R., & P.K. Fok. 2022. "Cultivating Students' Computational Thinking Through Student–Robot Interactions in Robotics Education." *International Journal of Technology and Design Education* 32 (4): 1983–2002.

Recchia, S., & V.I. Puig. 2018. "Early Childhood Teachers Finding Voice Among Peers: A Reflection on Practice." *The New Educator* 15 (8): 1–15.

Relkin, E., L.E. de Ruiter, & M.U. Bers. 2021. "Learning to Code and the Acquisition of Computational Thinking by Young Children." *Computers & Education* 169: 104222. doi:10.1016/j.compedu.2021.104222.

Resnick, M., J. Maloney, A. Moroy-Hernández, N. Rusk, E. Eastmond, K. Brennan, A. Millner, E. Rosenbaum, J. Siler, B. Silverman, & Y. Kafai. 2009. "Scratch: Programming for All." *Communications of the ACM* 52 (11): 60–67.

Resnick, M., & E. Rosenbaum. 2013. "Designing for Tinkerability." In *Design, Make, Play: Growing the Next Generation of STEM Innovators,* eds. M. Honey & D.E. Kanter, 163–81. Routledge.

Se, S., B. Ashwini, A. Chandran, & K.P. Soman. 2015. "Computational Thinking Leads to Computational Learning: Flipped Classroom Experiments in Linear Algebra." Paper presented at the International Conference on Innovations in Information, in Coimbatore, India. doi:10.1109/ICIIECS.2015.7193021.

Shute, V.J., C. Sun, & J. Asbell-Clarke. 2017. "Demystifying Computational Thinking." *Educational Research Review* 22: 142–58.

Sullivan, A., & M.U. Bers. 2013. "Gender Differences in Kindergarteners' Robotics and Programming Achievement." *International Journal of Technology and Design Education* 23 (3): 691–702.

Thornton, K., & S. Cherrington. 2018. "Professional Learning Communities in Early Childhood Education: A Vehicle for Professional Growth." *Professional Development in Education* 45 (3): 418–32.

Tucker, A. 2003. *A Model Curriculum for K–12 Computer Science: Final Report of the ACM K–12 Task Force Curriculum Committee.* Report. Association for Computing Machinery. https://dl.acm.org/doi/book/10.1145/2593247.

Vanover, S.T. 2020. "From Circle Time to Small Groups: Meeting Children's Needs." *Teaching Young Children* 13 (4): 28–29.

Vujičić, L., & A. Čamber Tambolaš. 2017. "Professional Development of Preschool Teachers and Changing the Culture of the Institution of Early Education." *Early Child Development and Care* 187 (10): 1583–95.

Vygotsky, L.S. 1986. *Thought and Language.* Trans. A. Kozulin. MIT Press.

Wang, C., J. Shen, & J. Chao. 2022. "Integrating Computational Thinking in STEM Education: A Literature Review." *International Journal of Science and Mathematics Education* 20 (8): 1949–72.

Wanless, S.B., & P.A. Crawford. 2016. "Reading Your Way to a Culturally Responsive Classroom." *Young Children* 71 (2): 8–15.

Wing, J.M. 2006. "Computational Thinking." *Communications of the ACM* 49 (3): 33–35.

Wing, J.M. 2008. "Computational Thinking and Thinking About Computing." *Philosophical Transactions of the Royal Society* 366 (1881): 3717–25.

Yang, W., H. Luo, & J. Su. 2022. "Towards Inclusiveness and Sustainability of Robot Programming in Early Childhood: Child Engagement, Learning Outcomes, and Teacher Perception." *British Journal of Educational Technology* 53 (6): 1486–510.

Yang, W., D.T.K. Ng, & H. Gao. 2022. "Robot Programming Versus Block Play in Early Childhood Education: Effects on Computational Thinking, Sequencing Ability, and Self-Regulation." *British Journal of Educational Technology* 53 (6): 1817–41.

Zeng, Y., W. Yang, & A. Bautista. 2023. "Computational Thinking in Early Childhood Education: Reviewing the Literature and Redeveloping the Three-Dimensional Framework." *Educational Research Review* 39: 100520. doi:10.1016/j.edurev.2023.100520.

Index

Page numbers followed by *b* and *f*, indicate boxes and figures, respectively.

N